NORMALITY AND PATHOLOGY IN CHILDHOOD

IN CHILDHOOD

Assessments of Development

NORMALITY AND PATHOLOGY IN CHILDHOOD

Assessments of Development

ANNA FREUD

with a new introduction by

DR. S. CLIFFORD B. YORKE

LONDON

KARNAC BOOKS

AND THE INSTITUTE OF PSYCHO-ANALYSIS

1989

First published in 1966
by The Hogarth Press
New edition published in 1980
Reprinted with their permission by
H. Karnac (Books) Ltd,
58 Gloucester Road,
London SW7 4QY
1989

British Library Cataloguing in Publication Data
Freud, Anna, 1895–1982
   Normality and pathology in childhood: assessments
of development.—Reprint of 2nd ed.
   1. Children. Psychological development. Assessment
   I. Title   II. Institute of Psycho-Analysis
   155.4

ISBN 0-946439-65-6

Printed in Great Britain by BPCC Wheatons Ltd, Exeter

Contents

Acknowledgments

Since the bulk of this book is based on clinical impressions gained in the various departments of the Hampstead Child-Therapy Clinic, I owe a great debt of gratitude to Miss Helen Ross, Dr. Muriel Gardiner, and Dr. K. R. Eissler for establishing, housing, and tirelessly assisting this organization, and to the Field Foundation, the Foundations Fund for Research in Psychiatry, the Freud Centenary Fund, the Grant Foundation, the Flora Haas Estate, the Newland Foundation, the Old Dominion Foundation, the William Rosenwald Family Fund, and the Taconic Foundation for their generous support over many years.

I owe a similar debt to the analysts and child therapists of the Clinic for placing the material of their child analyses at my disposal.

A section of the book, the "Metapsychological Profile of the Child" (contained in Chapter 4) was submitted to the National Institute for Mental Health in Washington in 1961 as a possible basis for further work within the Hampstead Clinic, and such an investigation under the title of "Assessment of Pathology in Childhood" has been supported since then by Public Health Service Grant No. M-5683, MH (1, 2, 3). Other sections of the book completed in connection with this project are: "The Concept of Developmental Lines" (in Chapter 3) and "Dissociality, Homosexuality, Perversion as Diagnostic Categories in Childhood" (in Chapter 5).

The sections of "Assessment of Childhood Disturbances" and the "Concept of Developmental Lines" have appeared as preliminary communications in *The Psychoanalytic Study of the Child*, Vols. XVII and XVIII; "Regression as a Principle in Mental Development" in the *Bulletin of the Menninger Clinic*, Vol. 27.

Introduction

For the educated general reader with an interest in
psychoanalysis, as well as the professional working
with child or adult, *Normality and Pathology in
Childhood* is arguably Anna Freud's most singly
important book. It is true that *The Ego and the
Mechanisms of Defence* (1936) has a special place in the
history of psychoanalysis, and perhaps in the reader's
mind and on his bookshelf. It appeared at, and helped
to mark, a point at which the psychology of the ego
was advancing by leaps and bounds, and though the
author has since elaborated and expanded on its
principal themes (Sandler *et al.*, 1980) its importance
has not been diminished by time. Its memorable
illustrations still make their points with telling effect.
But the present work, first published in 1965, has a
significance of a different order. If today, so many
years after its initial appearance, I were allowed to
possess only *one* book on psychoanalytic child psy-

chology, it would have to be *Normality and Pathology in Childhood*. No other single work addresses the development of the normative and the disturbed so comprehensively; and it does so without any artificial separation of the one from the other. It is firmly based on clinical observation and detailed study. It is remarkably compact, and simple and elegant in style; but the ease with which Anna Freud engages the reader should not be allowed to disguise the intricacies of what she has to say.

Yet in some ways it can be argued that Anna Freud's most important creation was not a book at all but the Clinic over which she presided for thirty years. What was once known by the familiar shorthand of "Hampstead" became, after her death in 1982, *The Anna Freud Centre*: and the book re-issued here must be firmly placed in space and time at a point in the Centre's evolution.

The development of this influential organization from its forerunner, the Hampstead War Nurseries, has been chronicled elsewhere (e.g., Yorke and Moran, 1989) and for present purposes only a few bare facts need be repeated. The War Nurseries were set up for the residential care of children whose families were dislocated—some irretrievably—by wartime conditions. But the Nurseries provided not only a very special service, but an opportunity to study through meticulous observations and careful records, significant aspects of child development and the impact on children of traumata involved in wartime separation. All this is fully described in two books by Anna Freud and Dorothy Burlingham: *Children in Wartime* (1942) and *Infants Without Families* (1944). When the war came to an end and the Nurseries were disbanded, many of its staff sought training in psychology or social work, and were employed in many of the post-war child guidance clinics that were starting to spring up; but the psychotherapy with children that they were called upon to do seemed to demand a more extensive and systematized training than they felt themselves to possess, and they had become convinced it should include personal analysis. Pressure was brought to bear on Anna Freud and her psycho-analytic colleagues, and in 1948 the Hampstead Child Training Course came into being, conducted in the homes of its instructors.

A course without a clinic to which referrals can be made labours under a considerable handicap, but it was only through the generosity of friends and bene-factors, particularly in the United States, that a house was eventually bought in Maresfield Gardens and a Centre established where children could be assessed diagnostically, offered psychoanalytic treatment where this was appropriate, studied in the interests of research into childhood development, and the basis provided for what became, as it expanded beyond all anticipation, the most comprehensive organization of its kind in the world.

The expansion took place on a number of fronts. The study and understanding of normal development was furthered through the foundation of a Well-Baby clinic, a Mother/Toddler group, and a Nursery School for under fives. From the standpoint of pathology an extensive and intensive diagnostic service provided

fresh material and new insights into a wide range of
childhood disturbances. The diagnostic services themselves became the source of refinements in psychoanalytic nosology and nosography, while special
groups were established for the study of clinical and
theoretical concepts. The need to organize a system of
indexing to facilitate research was devised by Dorothy
Burlingham (the co-founder of the clinic), enthusi-
astically supported by Anna Freud, and led to the
setting up of an Index group that came under the
chairmanship of Professor Joseph Sandler. The need to
refine and review conceptual thinking on psychoanalytic issues, fostered by the index, in time resulted
in significant publications, many of which appeared
over the years in *The Psychoanalytic Study of the
Child*.

But what must be emphasised in all this is Anna
Freud's unique way of working that drew the best out
of students and colleagues, and encouraged them to
cultivate and pursue their own special and specialized
interests in the broader framework of child psychoanalytic psychology. Many study groups were set up:
one of these, concerned with the role of sight in normal
development and the understanding of the blind,
sprang from Mrs Burlingham's unique creation of a
Nursery School for pre-school blind children. Others
included the study group for so-called borderline
children, for problems of delinquency, for physically
handicapped children, and many more. Although Anna
Freud never interfered in the work of these groups she
took the greatest interest in what they did and was
always available for consultation. In this she was

assisted by the system of detailed documentation first set up in the War Nurseries. Since everything that happened in the study groups, as well as in diagnostic assessment and in treatment, was comprehensively recorded, she was able, through these reports, to follow all the continuing work, and she retained their contents in a memory that can only be compared with her father's. But there was another and no less important advantage in the method: the observations drawn from these many sources were available for the use of all staff and students for whatever research or study plan they might wish to undertake. The habit of writing became ingrained even in those initially averse to it and, pressed into disciplined service, repeatedly led to valuable contributions to the literature.

The link between the Course and Clinic and the subject matter of *Normality and Pathology in Childhood* may already be apparent, but its timing was not, I believe, accidental. It was written at a point where psychoanalytic nosology had taken a fresh and revolutionary turn with the development of the diagnostic profile; and the concept of development lines, which in many ways complemented it (cf. Yorke, 1980), had also shown its value for assessing the suitability and readiness for children within the normative range to embark on fresh tasks and forward steps—such as placement in nursery school. Both of these valuable psychological tools play a major part in the book's expositions. Furthermore, the Index was by then firmly established, and a substantial number of cases treated analytically had been documented and classified

according to its principles—in a way, that is, that
made them readily available to a growing number of
research workers. The study group devoted to the
blind was beginning to influence the management of
such children in other organizations and special
schools. The Well-baby Clinic and the Nursery School
were firmly founded and contributing apace to the
understanding of the normative. Follow-up studies
were under way in spite of all the difficulties attendant
on such projects, and it had become possible to gauge
the accuracy of initial assessments of disturbed
children by later systematic re-assessment of those
who had been taken into analysis. Although the
Clinic's scientific progress was still actively developing in all fields, its progress up to that date needed to
be recorded and brought together in terms of the
principles on which it was based. *Normality and
Pathology in Childhood* reduced this mass of detail to
its essentials and summarized the more generalized
developments in a clear and assimilable form. It was
never intended to be a detailed account of the Clinic's
activities as such. But workers everywhere who
wished to follow similar directions or felt stimulated
to do so could maintain its scientific momentum
wherever they happened to be; while for the Clinic
itself the work's unifying function acted as a spring-
board for further developments. No one else could
have realized the task that Anna Freud undertook in
writing it; and several years after her death it fulfils
its original purpose and still acts as a catalyst to
workers everywhere.

But time did not stand still, either for Anna Freud

herself or for the Clinic in which she remained the
central figure. The fertile thinking that characterises
the book has resulted in a remarkable burst of energy
that not only influenced her colleagues but led Anna
Freud herself, in the last 15 or 20 years of her life, to
extend and develop her contributions. The newcomers
to this book, and those who approach it afresh, may
well wish to look at this later work in the light of what
was said at the time. It may be helpful to draw
attention to some of these later contributions so that
the reader can trace at leisure a continuous line of
thinking that has permanently enriched psychoanalytic psychology.

Anna Freud always thought it important to put the
insights gained from child analysis at the service of
adult work and understanding. This was reflected in a
number of later papers. *Some thoughts about the place
of psychoanalytic theory in the training of psychiatrists*
(1966) recorded an address to the Menninger
Foundation in which she observed that the extensive
facilities to be found there presented psychiatric
residents with "the full range of human problems as
they arise from the cradle to the grave". In discussing
the application of psychoanalytic thinking to work
with very disturbed patients, she again demonstrated
her knowledge of, and interest in, general psychiatry.
It was precisely this concern that led her to encourage
Thomas Freeman to adapt a Profile schema for the
assessment of psychosis, and she appealed to her child
therapist colleagues to join him and other adult
psychiatrists in an attempt to detect possible childhood forerunners of later psychotic disturbance.

The comparison between child and adult disturbances intrigued her; her thinking about it had influenced the form of the profile schema for adult assessment; and in discussing *Indications and Contra-Indications for Child Analysis* in 1968 she had drawn attention to some striking comparisons between her father's discussion of *Analysis Terminable and Interminable* (1937)—which was restricted to problems in adults that led to analytic difficulties—and upsets in childhood which resembled those in adults rather more closely than was often recognised. She pointed out that, although one might hesitate to take an adult into treatment if he was in the middle of a tempestuous love affair, it was important to remember that the child battling his way through the oedipus complex was enduring a comparable state of affairs. Although one would hesitate to take into analysis an adult immediately after an important bereavement, it was not always considered that a child whose mother had just given birth to a sibling might be in a similar state of object loss. Anna Freud returned to this theme in an address to the New York Psychoanalytic Society when she discussed *Difficulties in the Path of Psychoanalysis* (1968), and added, to the difficulties listed by Sigmund Freud in respect of adult patients, some special factors militating against success in the treatment of children.

Anna Freud continued to emphasize the importance of the childhood disturbances brought about by the frustration of developmental needs and its consequences. She drew attention to the differences between infantile neurosis, with its regressive moves and conflictual compromises, and those disturbances where conflicts, while still lodged internally, differ from those of the neuroses in that the influences they exert do not derive simply from the past but are "acute and ongoing". The most difficult group for which a decision to recommend analysis is singularly fraught is that in which damage is caused and maintained by active, continuing infuences lodged in the environment. The delineation of such pathology, which is not psychotic or even borderline, is of a different order from childhood neurosis, and may not respond to classical analysis except in terms of its neurotic superstuctures. Such cases may also call for what Anna Freud referred to as *developmental assistance*.

In the present context, the most important of her later contributions developing these lines of thought is to be found in her discussion of *The Symptomatology of Childhood* (1970) in which she set out what she described as "a preliminary attempt at classification". She tried to put child disturbances into a broad perspective, and emphasised that, since these are much less structured than the adult disorders, they are even less suited to traditional taxonomy than their grown-up counterparts. Although she was aware of "the misleading quality of manifest symptomatology" in children, she nevertheless took the view that analysts who attached little importance to the surface presentation might well be doing a disservice to diagnosis. She distinguished between symptoms proper and what she called "other signs of disturbance" or "other reasons for a child's clinical referral". In the first category she included symptoms resulting from inadequate differentiation between somatic and psychological processes—the "psychosomatics of early life", in which early psychic distress can be discharged through bodily channels, and bodily distress through psychic pain; symptoms resulting from compromise formations between id and ego, exemplified, say, by a childhood neurosis in which a paralyzed leg might symbolically gratify the instinctual wish for a penis, while the uselessness of the limb satisfied the defence against that wish; symptoms resulting from the eruption of id derivatives into the ego; and other important groups of symptoms including those resulting from undefended regression and those which have an underlying organic basis. In the second category—other signs of disturbance—she included a number of non-specific pointers to *underlying* disturbances such as the manifold fears and anxieties of childhood; delays or failures in development; the school failures, failures in social adaptation; and those various aches and pains which had psychological origins of varying type and severity. In her conclusions, she again drew attention to the value of the Profile in assessing these various disorders.

During the next ten years all these contributions to psychoanalytic assessment were subject to extension and elaboration in a variety of contexts. Anna Freud was at all times concerned with the applicability of diagnostic refinement to questions of prognosis, treatment, and management. In her concern about those disturbances which might yield to analytic intervention, and those which might not, she was at pains to clarify the distinction between what might loosely be called childhood neurosis on the one hand, and on the other, developmental disturbances where the pathology appeared to be of a different order. She recognised that these disturbances were protean in form and that each individual child needed the most thoroughgoing investigation if the type of developmental disturbance was to be usefully understood. Her own studies in this field, and those of her colleagues, ultimately led her to put forward an important concept which still calls for wider attention and further study. Her account of the new concept in 1979 concerned *Mental health and illness in terms of internal harmony and disharmony*. She viewed mental health in terms of a harmonious interaction between the inner agencies themselves—that is, between id, ego and superego—and between these agencies and outside influences. Such harmony can only be achieved if the inner agencies have at any particular time reached and maintained comparable levels of development and if the external influences with which they interact reflect an "average, expectable environment" (Hartmann, 1939). But she was at the same time aware that development was never really harmonious except in a maturational sense—that is, in terms of both quantitative and qualitative progress. Once adequate structuralization has taken place, the agencies are always in latent dispute.

So Anna Freud was not referring to *absence* of conflict. What she had in mind was "inner equilibrium" and she emphasised how hard it can be to achieve this "in the early years, when forces determining the child's development are external as well as internal" (1979). She pointed out that what called for integration with each other were "the potentialities inherent in the inherited constitution; the vicissitudes connected with the gradual structuralization of the personality; and the influences emanating from the parental environment which is reponsible for the atmosphere in which development proceeds". She considered that while this task was a difficult one under any circumstances, it could be managed if all or most of the responsible factors were within a normal range as far as "momentum and quality" were concerned and did not differ greatly from each other in terms of onset and rate of progression. Since however, innate dispositions, different patterns of individual growth, and very varied family backgrounds diverged so widely,this inner equilibrium was by no means a universal outcome. Constitutionally determined deviations, deviant modes of structuralization, and deviant environmental factors could all lead to a disharmonious result.

But disharmonies also arise from disturbances in development brought about by the breakdown of synchronization—that is, in premature or delayed advance of any one of the structures in relation to the others. Her examples make the point. Cannibalistic impulses and fantasies normally appear before there is any organised ego with which they might come into conflict. If they persist beyond that time, or face a critical ego activity that has set in prematurely, the situation is quite a different one. Again, archaic fears of darkness, of loneliness and of loud noises are not persistently troublesome if, at their height, the infant is assured of support, comfort and reassurance from his caring adults at a time when his reality sense is insufficiently developed to keep panic at bay. They become a much more serious danger to development if the child is neglected or if ego functioning occurs too slowly to allow the child to deal with them.

Again, if the child is refused the normal enjoyment of the anal phase, as may happen if such forms of drive expression are condemned by the parents or countered by too great an emphasis on toilet training and by excessive condemnation of aggression, the stage is set for ego controls which prematurely oppose drive development, and for precocious superego strictures. The result is a childhood foundation for a later obsessional personality if not an obsessional neurosis.

In Anna Freud's view, developmental disharmonies were not simply a matter of imbalances between the structures themselves, or the failure of the outside world to foster proper equilibrium. A developmental disharmony was integrated into the personality by the synthetic function of the ego. Anna Freud considered that, under these circumstances, the developmental disharmony is established "for better or for worse". If there were no possibility of early intervention before such a disharmony were established for good, analysis at a later date might well succeed in ameliorating any neurotic superstructure, but the disharmony itself might be very much less open to analytic influence.

Developmental disharmony was thought to be a basis for future mental disturbance rather than a specific disorder in its own right. It could form a breeding ground for neurosis, for various developmental disorders, and, in Freeman's view, for certain types of psychosis. Thus, its understanding seemed a necessary complement to what had been learned from psychoanalysis about the psychological contribution to psychiatric conditions of all kinds.

The reader of this book will not necessarily want to follow all these developments. The book itself remains a classic statement, marvelously self-contained. Its usefulness and value do not depend on later elaborations. But for those who do wish to follow some of the thinking that grew from it, these brief notes may provide something of a guideline to further enjoyments to come . However that may be, those who encounter the book for the first time have some pleasant surprises in store; while those who know it but do not possess it may very well want to give it a permanent and handy place on their working desk.

Clifford Yorke

British Psychoanalytical Society

Bibliography

FREUD, A. (1936). *The Ego and the Mechanisms of Defence.* London: Hogarth Press.

———— (1966). Some thoughts about the place of psycho-analytic theory in the training of psychiatrists. In: *Writings*, 7:59.72. New York: Int. Univ. Press

———— (1968a). Indications and contraindications for child analysis. In: *Writings*, 7:110–123. New York: Int. Univ. Press.

———— (1968b). Difficulties in the path of psychoanalysis: a confrontation of past with present viewpoints. In *Writings*, 7:124–156. New York: Int. Unvi. Press.

———— (1970). The symptomatology of childhood: a preliminary attempt at classification. In *Writings*, 7:157–188. New York: Int. Univ. Press.

———— (1979). Mental health and illness in terms of internal harmony and disharmony. In *Writings*, 8:110–118. New York: Int. Univ. Press.

FREUD, A. & BURLINGHAM, D. (1942). *Young Children in War Time: Two Years Work in a Residential War Nursery.* London: George Allen and Unwin.

———— (1944). *Infants without Families.* London: George

Allen and Unwin.

FREUD, S. (1937). Analysis terminable and Interminable. *S.E.* 23. 216–253. London: Hogarth Press.

HARTMANN, H. (1939). *Ego Psychology and the Problem of Adaptation.* New York: Int. Univ. Press.

SANDLER, J., KENNEDY, H. & TYSON, R. L. (1980). *The Technique of Child Psychoanalysis: Discussions with Anna Freud.* London: Hogarth Press. Cambridge, Mass.: Harvard Univ. Press.

YORKE, C. (1980). The contributions of the diagnostic profile and the assessment of developmental lines to child psychiatry. *Psychiat. Clinics N. America,* 3:593–603.

YORKE, C & MORAN, G. (1989). *The Freudian Tradition: the Work of the Anna Freud Centre.* In preparation.

Foreword to the 1980 edition

The circumstances of psychoanalytic training as well as the human material seen in psychoanalytic practice tend to deflect the analysts' interest from the normal and to tempt them to explore increasingly not only the riddles of the neuroses and character deformations but also those of the borderline cases, the delinquencies, the perversions and psychoses. It is not easy to reverse the direction of this trend and to capture instead one's colleagues' attention for the problems of ordinary personality growth and adaptation to reality.

Nevertheless, at least so far as child analysis is concerned, this seems to me to be the task of the future. It is not only the individual's sex- and love-life which have to pass through a series of stages, from birth onwards until adult status has been reached. A similar step-by-step path can be delineated also for all the other characteristics which are the hallmark of maturity. Although it may be tempting to imagine at least some of them as the result of peaceful growth,

1

child-analytic investigations reveal that this is not true for the majority. On the contrary, they are shown to be the end-points of arduous and conflictual developmental processes, not very different in their structure from the neurotic formations which are compromises between the demands of the internal and external world.

Much work remains to be done before a complete and detailed picture of personality growth can be assembled in this manner and *Normality and Pathology in Childhood* represents no more than a first determined step towards such an aim. That a new edition of this book is needed may be taken as a hopeful sign in the desired direction.

Anna Freud

London, July 1979

CHAPTER 1

The Psychoanalytic View of Childhood: Long-Distance and Close-Up

RECONSTRUCTIONS FROM THE ANALYSES OF ADULTS AND THEIR APPLICATIONS

Since the beginning of psychoanalysis, when the discovery was made that "Hysterics suffer mainly from reminiscences" (Breuer and Freud, 1893), analysts have been concerned more with the past of their patients than with their present experiences, and more with the era of growth and development than with maturity.

It was this preoccupation with the early happenings in life which raised hopes in many quarters that analysts would become experts on childhood, even when they were engaged in the therapy of adults only. Their knowledge of the processes of mental growth, and their understanding of the interplay between the external and internal forces which shape the individual, were expected to qualify them automatically for being knowledgeable in all instances where a child's emotional stability or normal functioning were in doubt.

So far as the earliest era of psychoanalytic work is concerned, a survey of the literature shows that little was done specifically to fulfill these hopes. At that time the efforts were devoted entirely to fact finding and to perfecting the technique which was unearthing such new facts as a sequence of libidinal phases (oral, anal, phallic), the oedipus and the castration complex, infantile amnesia, etc. Since these important discoveries owed their origin to deductions from the analyses of adults, the method of "reconstructing" childhood events was held in high esteem and was used consistently to produce more of the data which today form the core of psychoanalytic child psychology.

On the other hand, it did not take more than one or two decades of such work before a number of analytic authors ventured beyond the boundaries of fact finding and began to apply the new knowledge to the upbringing of children. The temptation to do so was almost irresistible. The therapeutic analyses of adult neurotics left no doubt about the detrimental influence of many parental and environmental attitudes and actions such as dishonesty in sexual matters, unrealistically high moral standards, overstrictness or overindulgence, frustrations, punishments, or seductive behavior. It seemed a feasible task to remove some of these threats from the next generation of children by enlightening parents and altering the conditions of upbringing, and to devise thereby what was called hopefully a "psychoanalytic education," serving the prevention of neurosis.

The attempts to reach this aim have never been abandoned, difficult and bewildering as their results turned out to be at times. When we look back over their history now, after a period of more than forty years, we see them as a long series of trials and errors. Much of the uncertainty which accompanied these experiments was inevitable. It was at that time not possible to have full insight into the whole complicated network of drives, affects, object relations, ego apparatuses, ego functions and defenses, internalizations and ideals, with the mutual interdependencies between id and ego and the resultant defects of development, regressions, anxieties, compromise formations, and character distortions. The body of psychoanalytic knowledge grew gradually, one small finding being added to the next. The application of the relevant data to the problems of upbringing and of prevention of mental illnesses had no option except to proceed equally step by step, always following closely in the same slow and laborious path. As new discoveries of pathogenic agents were made in clinical work or arrived at by the changes and innovations in theoretical thinking, they were lifted out, translated into warnings and precepts for parents and educators, and became part and parcel of psychoanalytic upbringing.

The sequence of these extrapolations is well known by now. Thus, at the time when psychoanalysis laid great emphasis on the seductive influence of sharing the parents' bed and the traumatic consequences of witnessing parental intercourse, parents were warned against bodily intimacy with their children and against performing the sexual act in the presence of even their youngest infants. When it was proved in the analyses of adults that the withholding of sexual knowledge was responsible for many intellectual inhibitions, full sexual enlightenment at an early age was advocated. When hysterical symptoms, frigidity, impotence, etc., were traced back to prohibitions and the subsequent repressions of sex in childhood, psychoanalytic upbringing put on its program a lenient and permissive attitude toward the manifestations of infantile, pregenital sexuality. When the new instinct theory gave aggression the status of a basic drive, tolerance was extended also to the child's early and violent hostilities, his death wishes against parents and siblings, etc. When anxiety was recognized as playing a central part in symptom formation, every effort was made to lessen the children's fear of parental authority. When guilt was shown to correspond to the tension between the inner agencies, this was followed by the ban on all educational measures likely to produce a severe superego. When the new structural view of the personality placed the onus for maintaining an inner equilibrium on the ego, this was translated into the need to foster in the child the development of ego forces strong enough to hold their own against the pressure of the drives.

Finally, in our time, when analytic investigations have turned to earliest events in the first year of life and highlighted their importance, these specific insights are being translated into new and in some respects revolutionary techniques of infant care.

Owing to this protracted and piecemeal elaboration, the fabric of psychoanalytic education could not but remain unsystematic at all times. Furthermore, its precepts changed direction repeatedly, emphasis being first on freedom for drive activity, then on ego strength, then again on the intactness of libidinal relations. In the unceasing search for pathogenic agents and preventive measures, it seemed always the latest analytic discovery which promised a better and more final solution of the problem.

Some of the pieces of advice given to parents over the years were consistent with each other; others were contradictory and mutually exclusive. Some proved beneficial, almost beyond expectation. Thus, analytic education can count among its successes the greater openness and confidence between parents and children which was arrived at after sexual matters were treated and discussed with greater honesty. Another victory was over the stubborn obstinacy of certain early ages which disappeared almost completely after the problems of the anal phase were recognized and bowel training was carried out later and less harshly. Also certain eating disturbances of children ceased to exist after infant feeding and weaning were altered to correspond more closely to the oral needs. Some sleeping disturbances (i.e., difficulties in falling asleep) were removed after the struggles against masturbation, thumb sucking, and other autoerotic activities were lessened.

On the other hand, there was no lack of disappointments and surprises. It was unexpected that even the most well-meant and simply worded sexual enlightenment was not readily acceptable to young children and that they persisted in clinging to what had to be recognized as their own sexual theories which translate adult genitality into the age-appropriate terms of orality and anality, violence and mutilation. It was equally unexpected that the disappearence of the masturbation conflict would have—besides its beneficial consequences—some unwanted side effects on character formation by eliminating struggles which, in spite of their pathogenic aspects, had served also as a moral training ground (Lampl-de Groot, 1950). Above all, to rid the child of anxiety proved an impossible task. Parents did their best to reduce the children's fear of them, merely to find that they were increasing guilt feelings, i.e., fears of the child's own conscience. Where, in its turn, the severity of the superego was reduced, children produced the deepest of all anxieties, i.e., the fear of human beings who feel unprotected against the pressure of their drives.

In short, in spite of many partial advances, psychoanalytic education did not succeed in becoming the preventive measure that it set out to be. It is true that the children who grew up under its influence were in some respects different from earlier generations; but they were not freer from anxiety or from conflicts, and therefore not less exposed to neurotic or other mental illnesses. Actually, this need not have come as a surprise if optimism and enthusiasm for preventive work had not triumphed with some authors over the strict application of psychoanalytic tenets. There is, according to the latter, no wholesale "prevention of neurosis." The very division of the personality into an id, ego, and superego presents us with the picture of a psychic structure in which each part has its specific derivation, its specific aims and allegiances, and its specific mode of functioning. By definition, the various psychic agencies are at cross-purpose with each other, and this gives rise to the inner discords and clashes which reach consciousness as mental conflicts. These latter exist therefore wherever complex structural personality development has come into being. There are of course instances where an "analytic upbringing" helps the child toward finding adequate solutions which safeguard mental health; but there are also many others where inner disharmony cannot be prevented and becomes the starting point for one or the other kind of pathological development.

THE ADVENT OF CHILD ANALYSIS
AND ITS CONSEQUENCES

Some of the doubts and uncertainties governing the field were dispelled with the introduction of the analysis of children. Psychoanalysis moved a step nearer to providing what it had set out to provide from the beginning: a service of child experts.

There was from then onwards an additional source of material for the systematic building up of a psychoanalytic child psychology, and the integration of the two kinds of data, direct and reconstructed, became a. rewarding task. While reconstruction of childhood events from the analyses of adults kept its place, reconstructions from the analyses of older children and findings from analysis of the youngest were added to it. But child analysis provided more than this. Besides studying the "interaction between the concrete environment and the development of the child's capacities," it opened up a "host of intimate data about the child's life," so that "his fantasies as well as his daily experiences became accessible to observation . . . only the child analyst provided a setting in which daydreams and night-fears, games and productive expressions of the child became understandable . . . in a much more concrete sense than the secret parts of a child's experiences . . . had ever before become accessible to adult understanding."[1] Also, in the analyses of the young, the infantile complexes and the tur-

[1] The quotations are taken from Ernst Kris (1950, p. 28); see also Ernst Kris (1951).

moil created by them in the mind were found to be more open to view, not yet shut off from consciousness by amnesia or distorted by the later action of cover memories.

The close-up view of childhood which developed over the years on the basis of child analytic work provides for the child analyst an approach to personality development which differs subtly from that of those colleagues who see children through the medium of the adult only. Child analysts, therefore, offer not only welcome confirmations of analytic assumptions, as they had been expected to do from the outset; they also help toward providing decisions where "alternative hypotheses had been advanced by reconstructive methods."[2] They succeed in altering the emphasis laid on particular points and in correcting perspectives (see A. Freud, 1951). And finally, as I hope to show in what follows later, they make their own contribution to metapsychology and the theory of psychoanalytic therapy.

DIRECT CHILD OBSERVATION IN THE SERVICE OF PSYCHOANALYTIC CHILD PSYCHOLOGY

In their theoretical writings it took analysts some time to "come to the conclusion that psychoanalytic psychology" (and especially psychoanalytic child psychology) "is not limited to what can be gained through the use of the psychoanalytic method" (Heinz Hartmann, 1950a). Not so in action. Following the publication of the *Three Essays on the Theory of Sex* (S. Freud, 1905), the first generation of analysts had already begun to watch and report their children's behavior with regard to the details of infantile

[2] Ernst Kris (1950), quoting Robert Waelder (1936).

sexuality, the oedipus and castration complexes. Analyzed nursery school teachers, school teachers, and those working with adolescents, delinquents, and young criminals carried on this work in the 1920s and '30s, long before such work developed into the systematic enterprises they became after the Second World War.[3]

Nevertheless, as regards observational work outside the analytic setting, the analyst who habitually deals with repressed and unconscious materials has to overcome misgivings before he can extend his interest to surface behavior. In this respect it may be useful to review the relations between psychoanalysis and direct observation[4] as they have developed over the years. The question whether the latter, namely, direct scrutiny of the surface of the mind, can penetrate into the structure, functioning, and content of the personality has been answered at different times in different ways, but, especially so far as insight into child development is concerned, with increasing positiveness. Although there is no clear historical sequence which can be traced, there are several aspects and factors which, partly consecutively and partly simultaneously, have been of relevance in this respect.

The Analyst's Exclusive Concentration on the Hidden Depth

In the earliest period of psychoanalytic work, and long before child analysis came into being, there was a strong

[3] See Bernfeld, Aichhorn, Alice Balint, A. Freud, as well as the numerous publications in the *Zeitschrift für psychoanalytische Pädagogik*. Vienna: Internationaler Psychoanalytischer Verlag, 1927-1937.

[4] See also Heinz Hartmann (1950a).

tendency to keep the relations between analysis and surface observation wholly negative and hostile. This was the time of the discovery of the unconscious mind and of the gradual evolvement of the analytic method, two directions of work which were inextricably bound up with each other. It was then the task of the analytic pioneers to stress the difference between observable behavior and hidden impulses rather than the similarities between them and, more important than that, to establish the fact in the first instance that there existed such hidden, i.e., unconscious, motivation. Furthermore, this work had to be carried out in the face of opposition from a public who refused to believe in the existence of an unconscious to which consciousness had no free access, or in the possibility that factors could influence the mind without being open to view for the observer. Lay people especially were inclined to mistake the painstaking elaborations of material within the analytic process for an alleged uncanny ability of analysts to see the innermost secrets of a stranger at a glance, and persisted in this belief in spite of all protestations that the analyst is tied to his own laborious and slow method of observation and sees no more without it than the bacteriologist, deprived of his microscope, sees of bacilli with his naked eye. Psychiatric clinicians too were known to neglect the differences, for example, between the manifest occurrence of rape of a female child by her psychotic father and the unconscious latent strivings of the oedipus complex, and to call the former, instead of the latter, a "Freudian fact." In a famous criminal case of the time,[5] a judge even used the ubiquity of death wishes of sons against their fathers as an indict-

[5] The Halsmann case. See S. Freud (1931).

ment, without taking into account the mental alterations which are needed to allow unconscious and repressed impulses to become conscious intent and to be discharged into action. Academic psychologists, in their turn, attempted to verify or disprove the validity of the oedipus complex by inquiry and questionnaire, that is, by methods which by their very nature are unable to penetrate the barriers between the conscious and unconscious mind, and thereby to disclose in adults the repressed residues of infantile emotional strivings.

Nor was the younger generation of analysts of that period completely free of inclinations to confuse the content of the unconscious with its overt derivatives. In the psychoanalytic training courses on dream interpretation, for example, it remained for years one of the most difficult tasks for the instructors to teach differentiation between the latent and the manifest content of a dream and to impress on the students' understanding that the unconscious dream wish itself will not appear on the surface undisguised by the dream work, and that the conscious dream text is representative of the hidden content in an indirect manner only. Moreover, in their eagerness to reach beyond the confines of consciousness and to bridge the gap between surface and depth, many tried to spot from surface manifestations the sufferer from specific unconscious impulses, incestuous or sadomasochistic fantasies, castration anxieties, death wishes, etc., attempts which at the time were not feasible and therefore were misleading. It is not surprising that under conditions of this kind, all students of psychoanalysis were warned of such attempts at surface observation, were taught not to bypass patient analytic unraveling of the repressions, and to have no dealings with methods which could only constitute threats to the analysts' principal task of perfecting the analytic technique itself.

The Derivatives of the Unconscious as Material for Observation

In the same period, or slightly after it, there were other discoveries and factors at work which served to modify this uncompromising attitude toward surface observation. After all, what the analyst was exploring for the purpose of his therapeutic intervention was not the unconscious mind itself but its derivatives. The analytic setting, of course, contains the specific arrangements which invite and further the production of such derivatives by means of the complete relaxation to which the patient is submitted—the suspension of his critical faculties which makes free association possible, the exclusion of motility which enables even the most dangerous impulses to be verbalized harmlessly, the offer of the analyst's person for the transference of past experience, etc. But notwithstanding the fact that with the help of these technical arrangements the derivatives of the unconscious are more prolific and become manifest in a more orderly sequence, break-throughs from the depth and irruptions into the conscious mind are not confined to analytic sessions. To the degree to which the analyst became aware of their ubiquity, he became inclined also to include them as "material." With adults, there are the slips of the tongue, the faulty and symptomatic actions which reveal preconscious or unconscious impulses; there are the dream symbols and typical dreams which can be translated into their hidden meaning without interpretative work. With children, better still, there are simple fulfillment dreams which reveal the underlying wishes; there are also the conscious daydreams which give information about the daydreamer's libidinal development with minimal distortions. Examples of the latter are the heroic and rescue fantasies which show a boy at the height of his masculine strivings; the family romance and twin fantasies (Dorothy Burlingham, 1952) which characterize a latency child as being in the process of disillusionment with his parents; the beating fantasies which give evidence of fixation to the sadomasochistic, anal stage of infantile sexuality.

There have always been analysts who are more adept than others at using such manifest signs for guessing at unconscious content. Occasionally, they are endangered by this as therapists, since the ease with which they can translate clues may tempt them to proceed without the full cooperation of the patient, to make short cuts to the unconscious and to ignore resistances—a procedure which runs counter to the best traditions of analysis. But the same flair for the unconscious which can turn a correct analytic therapist into a "wild" analyst is a most useful attribute for the analytic observer who, by means of it, will turn otherwise arid and unrewarding surface manifestations into meaningful material.

The Defense Mechanisms as Material for Observation

The manifest appearance of children and adults became even more transparent for the analyst when attention was extended from the content and the derivatives of the unconscious mind, i.e., from the impulses, fantasies, images, etc., to the methods employed by the ego to keep them warded off from consciousness. Although these mechanisms are automatic and not conscious in themselves, the results achieved by them are manifest and easily accessible to the observer's view.

Of course, so far as the ego mechanism under scrutiny is *repression*, pure and simple, nothing becomes visible on the surface except the absence of trends which, according to the analyst's conception of normality, are required ingredients of the personality. Where, for example, a little girl is described by her parents as an "affectionate, undemanding, uncomplaining little thing," the analyst will note the conspicuous absence of the usual greed and aggression of childhood. Where parents stress an older sibling's "love for babies," the analyst will look for the fate of the absent jealousies. Where a child is correctly described by the parents as "incurious and not interested in matters such as the differences between sexes, the origin of babies, the relationship between the parents," it is obvious to us that an inner battle has been fought which has led to the conscious extinction of normal sexual curiosity, etc.

Fortunately, there are the other defense mechanisms which yield more tangible results for the observer. First among these are the *reaction formations* which, by definition, bring the repressed counterpart of the overtly displayed manifestation to the observer's notice. The overconcern of a little boy "whenever his father has to leave the house at night, in fog conditions," etc., is a certain pointer to his repressed death wishes; so is a child's anxious listening at night for the breathing of the siblings who inadvertently "might have died in their sleep." The qualities of shame, disgust, pity are known not to be acquired by any child except as results of internal struggles with exhibitionism, messing, cruelty; their appearance on the surface, therefore, is a valuable diagnostic pointer to the fate of these components of the drives. Similarly, the *sublimations* are retranslated fairly easily into the significant primitive impulses from which they are displaced. *Projections* in young children betray their sensitivity to a multitude of unwanted qualities and attitudes, etc.

Taught by the experiences gained within the analytic setting, analysts also became increasingly alerted to particular manifest combinations of attitudes, i.e., personality types which can be singled out with the naked eye and from which valid inferences can be drawn. This path to understanding was opened up first by insight into the genetic roots of the obsessional character, where the manifest appearance of orderliness, cleanliness, obstinacy, punctuality, parsimoniousness, indecisiveness, hoarding, collecting, etc., betrays the unconscious anal-sadistic trends from which they are fashioned. There was no reason why this particular constellation, although studied first, should remain unique in supplying instructive links between surface and depth. It was only reasonable to share the expectation "that other character traits as well will turn out similarly to be precipitates or reaction-formations related to particular pregenital structures" (S. Freud, 1932).

In fact, since 1932, when the quoted passage was written, many such expectations have been fulfilled, especially with regard to the oral and urethral character types, and especially with regard to children. If a child shows the attributes of insatiableness, greed, craving, is clinging, demanding, devouring in his relationships; or if he develops fears of being poisoned, food refusals, etc.—it is obvious to us that the point in his development from which danger arises and threatens his progress, i.e., his fixation point, lies in the oral phase. If he displays burning ambitiousness coupled with impulsive behavior, we place his fixation point in the urethral area. In all these instances, the links between the repressed id content and the manifest ego structures are so fixed and immutable that a mere glance at the surface is sufficient to allow the analyst to make accurate guesses as to what happens, or has happened, in the otherwise hidden layers of the mind.

Items of Childhood Behavior as Material for Observation

There emerged over the years "a growing awareness of the sign- or signal-function [which] behavior details may have for the observer" (Hartmann, 1950a). As a by-product of child analysis many of the child's actions and preoccupations have become transparent by now so that, when observed, they can be translated into the unconscious counterpart from which they are derived. Especially the transparency of the reaction formations has encouraged analytic workers to collect additional items which have equally fixed and unalterable links with specific id urges and their derivatives.

Taking as starting point once more the fact that *orderliness, time sense, cleanliness, unaggressiveness* are unmistakable pointers to bygone conflicts with anal strivings, it is possible to pinpoint similar indicators for conflict in the phallic phase. There are *shyness* and *modesty* which are reaction formations and as such complete reversals of former exhibitionistic tendencies; there is, further, the behavior described commonly as *buffoonery* or *clowning* which, in analysis, has been revealed as a distortion of phallic exhibitionism, with the showing off displaced from an asset of the individual to one of his defects. *Exaggerated manliness* and *noisy aggression* are overcompensations which betray underlying castration fears. Complaints about being *maltreated* and *discriminated against* are a transparent defense against passive fantasies and wishes. When a child complains about excessive *boredom*, we can be certain that he has forcibly suppressed his masturbation fantasies or masturbatory activities.

Observation of a child's behavior during bodily illness also permits conclusions as to his inner mental state. An ill child may turn for comfort to his environment, or away from it toward solitude and sleep; whether he chooses the former or the latter type of reaction betrays something of the state of his *narcissism* measured against the relative strength of his *attachment to the object world*. Meek submission in illness to doctor's orders, to dietary and motor restrictions, etc., which is often mistakenly attributed to a supposed reasonableness of the child, is due either to the regressive pleasure in being passively cared for and loved or is the result of *guilt feelings*, i.e., of the child's conception of illness as self-induced, well-deserved *punishment*. When an ill child anxiously looks after himself in a *hypochondriacal* manner, this is a certain indication that he feels badly mothered and is dissatisfied with the care and protection given to him by his environment.

Even observation of the child's typical play activities and games is productive of inside information. The well-known sublimatory occupations of *painting, modeling, water and sand play* point back to anal and urethral preoccupation. The dismantling of toys because of the wish to know what is *inside* betrays sexual curiosity. It is even significant in which manner a small boy plays with his railway: whether his main pleasure is derived from staging crashes (as symbols of parental intercourse); whether he is predominantly concerned with building tunnels and underground lines (expressing interest in the inside of the body); whether his cars and buses have to be loaded heavily (as symbols of the pregnant mother); or whether speed and smooth performance are his main concern (as symbols of phallic efficiency). A school boy's favorite position on the *football field* betrays something of his intimate relations to his contemporaries in the symbolic language of attack, defense, ability or inability to compete, to succeed, to adopt the active masculine role, etc. A little girl's *horse-craze* betrays either her primitive autoerotic desires (if her enjoyment is confined to the rhythmic movement on the horse); or her identification with the caretaking mother (if she enjoys above all looking after the horse, grooming it, etc.); or her penis envy (if she identifies with the big, powerful animal and treats it as an addition to her body); or her phallic sublimations (if it is her ambition to master the horse, to perform on it, etc.).

The behavior of children toward *food* reveals more to the knowing observer than a mere "fixation to the oral phase," to which the majority of food fads are commonly ascribed and of which the child's greediness is the most obvious manifest representative. If looked for in detail, there are other equally revealing items. Above all, since the disturbances of eating are developmental ones,[6] tied to particular phases and levels of id and ego growth, their detailed observation and exploration fulfill the sign- or signal-function of behavior details to perfection.

[6] See Chapter 5.

There remains the area of *clothes* from which other valuable clues can be extracted. It is well known that exhibitionism can be displaced from the body to its coverings and appear on the surface in the form of vanity. If repressed and reacted against, it appears as neglect in matters of dress. Undue sensitivity with regard to stiff and "scratchy" materials points to repressed skin erotism. In girls, dislike of their feminine anatomy reveals itself as avoidance of feminine clothes, frills, adornment, or as the opposite: as excessive wishes for showy, expensive dresses.

This multitude of attitudes, attributes, and activities is displayed openly by the child, all over the place in his home and school life and in whatever setup is chosen by the observer. Since each item is tied genetically to the specific drive derivative which has given rise to it, they permit direct conclusions to be drawn from the child's behavior to some of the concerns and conflicts which play a central role in his hidden mind.

In fact, there is such a profusion of behavioral data which can be turned to good account in the mind of the analytically schooled observer, that child analysts have to be warned not to be led astray by them. For one, deductions of this kind are not for therapeutic use; or, to express it more forcefully even: they are useless therapeutically. To make them the basis of symbolic interpretation would equal ignoring the ego defenses which are built up against the unconscious content, and this means increasing the patient's anxieties, heightening his resistances, in short, committing the technical error of bypassing analytic interpretation proper.

Secondly, the extent of such insight must not be overrated. Side by side with the behavior items which have become transparent, there is a multitude of others which are

derived not from one specific invariable source but sometimes from one, at other times from another underlying
impulse, without being linked specifically to any one of
them. Without exploration during analysis, these forms of
behavior remain therefore inconclusive.

The Ego under Observation

While in the areas and from the aspects described above,
the direct observer finds himself at a disadvantage compared with the practicing analyst, his status improves decisively with the inclusion of ego psychology into psychoanalytic work. So far as ego and superego are conscious
structures, direct, i.e., surface, observation becomes an appropriate tool of exploration, in addition to and in cooperation with exploration of the depth.

There is, for one, no controversy about the use of observation outside the analytic session with regard to the conflict-
free sphere of the ego, that is, the various *ego apparatuses*
which serve sensation and perception. Notwithstanding the
fact that the result of their action is of the utmost importance for internalization, identification, and superego formation, i.e., for processes which are accessible only in analytic
work, they themselves and the degree of maturation reached
by them are measurable from the outside.

Further, so far as the *ego functions* are concerned, the
analyst is served in almost equal measure by observation
inside and outside the analytic setting. The child's *ego
control over the motor functions* and his development of
speech, for example, can be assessed by simple observation.
Memory is measured by tests, so far as efficiency and range
are concerned, while analytic investigation is needed to

measure its dependence on the pleasure principle (to remember the pleasurable and forget the unpleasurable). The intactness or defects of *reality testing* are revealed in behavior. The *synthetic function,* on the other hand, works behind the scenes, and damage to it has to be traced in analysis except in the most severe instances of failure when it becomes obvious.

Observations of the surface and the depth complement each other also with regard to such vital aspects as the modes of mental functioning. The discovery of a primary and secondary process, the former governing dream work and symptom formation, the latter rational conscious thought, is due to analytic work, of course. But once established and described, the difference between the two processes can be seen also at a glance, for example, in extra-analytic observation of infants in the second year of life, or of preadolescents and adolescents with delinquent leanings. In both types of children quick alternations between the two modes of functioning are open to view: in times of mental quiescence behavior is governed by the secondary process; whenever an impulse (for sexual satisfaction, for attack, for possession) becomes urgent, primary process functioning takes over.

Finally, there are those areas of work where direct observation, as contrasted with analytic exploration, becomes the method of choice. There are limitations to analysis,[7] set on the one hand by the means of communication which are at the disposal of the child, and on the other hand by what is recoverable in the analytic transference of adults and can be used to reconstruct infantile experience. There is, above all, no very certain path which leads from analysis into the

[7] See also Heinz Hartmann (1950a).

preverbal period. Here, in recent years, direct observation has added much to the analyst's knowledge concerning the mother-child relationship and the impact of environmental influences during the first year of life. Moreover, the various forms of early separation anxiety became visible for the first time in residential institutions, crèches, hospitals, etc., not in analysis. Such insights are on the credit side of direct observation. On the other hand, it has to be noted on the debit side that none of these discoveries were made before the observers were analytically trained, and that the most vital facts such as the sequence of libido development and the infantile complexes, in spite of their manifest derivatives, remained unnoticed by direct observers until they were reconstructed from analytic work.

There are also areas where spot observation, longitudinal study, and child analysis work in combination. We get the fullest information if detailed recordings of an infant's behavior are followed by analysis in later childhood and the results compared; or if the analysis of a young child serves as an introduction to a detailed longitudinal study of manifest behavior. It is an added advantage that in such experiments the two methods (analytic versus direct observation) serve as a much needed check-up on each other.[8]

[8] See in this respect the studies undertaken by Ernst and Marianne Kris in the Child Study Center, Yale University, U.S.A., and in the Hampstead Child-Therapy Clinic, London, England.

CHAPTER 2

The Relations Between
Child Analysis and
Adult Analysis

THE THERAPEUTIC PRINCIPLES

Although the differences between child analysis[1] and adult analysis came into focus gradually, the child analysts themselves were in no hurry to proclaim the independence of their procedure from the classical technique. On the contrary, the tendency was definitely to emphasize the similarity or near-identity of the two processes.

It seemed almost a matter of prestige for those analysts who were also engaged in treating children to maintain that they felt bound by the same therapeutic principles[2] to

[1] Whatever is said here and in what follows about child analysis refers only to that type of it with which I am connected, not to any other variety or technique or to the theories derived from it.
[2] See Edward Bibring (1954).

25

which they were committed in the analysis of adults. Translated into terms of child analysis, these principles implied

   (i) not to make use of authority and to eliminate thereby as far as possible suggestion as an element of treatment;

  (ii) to discard abreaction as a therapeutic tool;

 (iii) to keep manipulation (management) of the patient to a minimum, i.e., to interfere with the child's life situation only where demonstrably harmful or potentially traumatic (seductive) influences were at work;

 (iv) to consider the analysis of resistance and transference, and interpretation of unconscious material as the legitimate tools of therapy.

With the technique of child analysis governed by these considerations, the child analysts could feel satisfied that there was no better definition of their actions than that used for classical analysis: to analyze ego resistance before id content and to allow the work of interpretation to move freely between id and ego, following the emergence of material; to proceed from the surface to the depth; to offer the person of the analyst as a transference object for the revival and interpretation of unconscious fantasies and attitudes; to analyze impulses so far as possible in the state of frustration and to avoid their being acted out and gratified; to expect relief of tension not from catharsis, but from the material being lifted from the level of primary process functioning to secondary thought processes; in short: to turn id into ego content.

THE CURATIVE TENDENCIES

But even if child analysis is at one with adult analysis with regard to the principles which underlie the handling of the situation, child analysis differs from adult analysis where other basic conditions of therapy are concerned. According to a useful formulation by E. Bibring (1937), psychoanalysis with adults owes its therapeutic successes to the liberation of particular forces which are present normally within the structure of the personality and work spontaneously in the direction of a cure. These "curative tendencies," as E. Bibring called them, if assisted by treatment, are harnessed to the analytic aim. They are represented by the patient's innate urges to complete development, to reach drive satisfaction, and to repeat emotional experience; by his preference for being normal rather than abnormal; by his ability to assimilate and integrate experience; and to externalize onto objects parts of his own personality.

It is precisely in this area that children differ from adults, and these differences are bound to affect the therapeutic reactions in the two types of treatment. The adult neurotic patient strives for *normality* since this holds out to him the promise of pleasure in sex and success in work, while the child patient may see "getting well" in the unpleasurable terms of having to adapt to an unpalatable reality and to give up immediate wish fulfillments and secondary gains. The adult's tendency to *repeat*, which is important for creating transference, is complicated in the child by his hunger for *new experience* and new objects. *Assimilation* and *integration*, which are essential helps in the phase of "working through," are counteracted in the child by the age-adequate emphasis on opposite mechanisms such as *denial, projection, isolation, splitting of the ego*. The urge to obtain *drive satisfaction*, which accounts for the upsurges from the id and is indispensable for the production of material in general, is so strong in children that it becomes an embarrassment rather than an asset in analysis. In fact, child analysis would receive very little help from the curative forces if it were not for one exception which restores the balance. By definition, and owing to the processes of maturation, the urge to *complete development* is immeasurably stronger in the immature than it can ever be in later life. With the neurotic adult, quantities of libido and aggression, together with the countercathexes against them, are locked up in his symptomatology; new drive energy, as soon as produced, is forced into the same direction. In contrast, the child's unfinished personality is in a fluid state. Symptoms which serve as conflict solutions on one level of development prove useless on the next and are discarded. Libido and aggression are in constant motion and more ready than in adults to flow into the new channels which are opened up by analytic therapy. In fact, where pathology is not too severe, the child analyst often will query after the successful conclusion of a treatment how much of the improvement he can claim as outcome of his therapeutic measures and how much he must ascribe to maturation and to spontaneous developmental moves.

TECHNIQUE

Compared with such essential issues, the much-discussed differences of technique between adult and child analysis seem almost of secondary importance. It is to be expected that, owing to their immaturity, children lack many of the qualities and attitudes which, in adults, are held to be indispensable for carrying out an analysis: that they have no insight into their abnormalities; that accordingly they do not develop the same wish to get well and the same type of treatment alliance; that, habitually their ego sides with their resistances; that they do not decide on their own to begin, to continue, or to complete treatment; that their relationship to the analyst is not exclusive, but includes the parents who have to substitute for or supplement the child's ego and superego in several respects. Any history of child analysis is more or less synonymous with the history of efforts to overcome and counteract these difficulties.

The Absence of Free Association

The childhood characteristics mentioned above, important as they are, play a minor part in the variation of technique from adult to child analysis, compared with one major factor: the child's inability or unwillingness to produce free associations. Children may tell dreams and daydreams as adults do, but without free association there is no reliable path from manifest to latent content. They may communicate verbally, after initial hesitations, but without free association this does not carry them beyond the confines of the conscious mind. This uncompromising attitude toward free association is to be found in all children, whether they do not trust their own ego strength sufficiently to suspend censorship or whether they do not trust adults enough to be honest with them.

To my mind, no remedy for this lack has been discovered over the years. Play with toys, drawing, painting, staging of fantasy games, acting in the transference have been introduced and accepted in place of free association and, *faute de mieux*, child analysts have tried to convince themselves that they are valid substitutes for it. In truth, they are nothing of the kind. It is one disadvantage that some of these modes of behavior produce mainly symbolic material and that this introduces into child analysis the element of doubt, uncertainty, arbitrariness which are inseparable from symbolic interpretation in general. Another disadvantage lies in the fact that under the pressure of the unconscious the child *acts* instead of talking, and this unfortunately introduces limits into the analytic situation. While the freedom of verbal association accompanied by restraint of motility is literally limitless, the same principle cannot be adhered to as soon as motor action in or outside the transference comes into question. Where the child endangers his own or the analyst's safety, severely damages property or tries to seduce or enforce seduction, the child analyst cannot help interfering, in spite of the greatest forbearance and the best intentions to the opposite, and even though the most vital material emerges in this manner. Words, thoughts, and fantasies equal dreams in their lack of impact on reality, while actions belong in a different category. It is no help to promise child patients that they can let all restraints go in the analytic hour and—parallel to the license to talk given in adult analysis—"*do* as they want." The child will soon convince the analyst that such freedom of action is not feasible and that the promise cannot be kept.

Another difference between the two techniques suggests itself, a difference to which so far no attention has been paid. While free association seems to liberate in the first instance the sexual fantasies of the patient, free action— even if only comparatively free—acts in a parallel way on the aggressive trends. What children overwhelmingly act out in the transference are therefore their aggressions, or the aggressive side of their pregenitality which prompts them to attack, hit, kick, spit, and provoke the analyst. Technically this creates difficulties, since valuable treatment time must often be spent in efforts to check excesses of aggression which analytic tolerance has released initially. Theoretically this linkage between acting out and aggression may produce a biased picture of the proportion between libido and aggression in the child.

That acting out which does not lead to interpretation, or for which interpretation is not accepted, is not beneficial is an undisputed fact, of course. Although age adequate as an expression and therefore normal, it does not lead to insight or to change. But beliefs to the contrary, which are residues of the cathartic period of analysis, have persisted in child analysis in some places long after they were discarded for the analysis of adults.

Interpretation and Verbalization

That the analyst's task to interpret unconscious material is the same with children and adults is a statement which needs some amendment and clarification. It is true, obviously, in one respect. With children, too, the aim of analysis remains the widening of consciousness without which ego control cannot be increased. This aim has to be reached, even if technical obstacles such as the absence of free association and the intensity of acting out increase the difficulty to do so.

The difference between the two techniques lies not in the aim but in the type of material which comes up to be interpreted. With adults, analysis deals for long stretches with material under secondary repression, that is, with the undoing of defenses against id derivatives which have been rejected from consciousness at one time or another. Only from there does it proceed to elements under primary repression, which are preverbal, have never formed part of the organized ego, and cannot be "remembered," only relived within the transference. Although this procedure is the same with older children, it is different with the youngest where the proportion between elements of the first and second kind and also the order of their appearance in analysis are reversed.

The ego of the young child has the developmental task to master on the one hand orientation in the external world and on the other hand the chaotic emotional states which exist within himself. It gains its victories and advances whenever such impressions are grasped, put into thoughts or words, and submitted to the secondary process.

For a variety of reasons, young children come into analytic treatment with this development delayed or uncompleted. With them, the process of interpretation proper goes hand in hand with verbalizing numerous strivings which as such are not incapable of consciousness (i.e., under primary repression) but have not yet succeeded in achieving ego status, consciousness, and secondary elaboration.

The importance of their verbalization for early development has been emphasized especially by Anny Katan (1961) who stresses that the date when superego formation takes place depends to a certain extent on the date when the small child acquires the ability to substitute secondary process thinking for primary process thinking; that verbalization is known to be the indispensable prerequisite for secondary process thinking; that verbalizing the perceptions of the external world precedes verbalizing the content of the internal world; and that this latter, in turn, promotes reality testing and ego control over id impulses. In fact, insight into the role that verbalization plays in development is by no

means new in analysis; we find it remarked on first in the
following quotation: "the man who first flung a word of
abuse at his enemy instead of a spear was the founder of
civilization" (S. Freud, 1893, p. 36).

While verbalization as part of interpretation of the repressed unconscious belongs to the analyses of all ages,
verbalization in the above sense plays a specific role in the
analyses of all children who enter analysis at a very early
age and state of development or with severe delays, arrests,
or defects of ego development.

Resistances

As regards resistance, the initial hopes were not fulfilled
that the child analyst would have easy play in this respect.
The child's unconscious did not prove to be less strictly
separated from consciousness than it is with adults. The
upsurge of id derivatives to the surface and into the analytic
session was not easier to bring about. On the contrary, the
forces opposing analysis are, if anything, stronger with children than with adult patients.

Resistances in adult analysis are surveyed usually according to the inner processes or agencies which give rise to
them. The *ego* resists analysis to safeguard the defenses
without which the warded off unpleasure, anxiety, and guilt
have to be faced again. The *superego* opposes analytic license
for thoughts and fantasies as threats to its existence. *Drive
derivatives* within or outside the transference, although released by the analytic process, act as resistances against it
if they press for fulfillment in action instead of stopping
short when they have served the purpose of insight. The *id*

as such resists change since it is tied to the principle of repetition.

Children share all these legitimate resistances with the adult, some of them intensified, varied, and extended. They add, further, several difficulties and obstacles which are specific for the internal and external situation of a developing individual.

(i) Since the child does not enter analysis of his own free will, and makes no contract with the analyst, he does not feel bound by any analytic rules.

(ii) Since the child does not take a long-term view of any situation, the discomfort, strain, and anxiety caused by the treatment in the present weigh more heavily with him than the idea of future gain.

(iii) Since age-adequately, the child acts in preference to talking, "acting out" dominates the analysis, except with obsessional children.[3]

(iv) Since the child's immature ego is insecurely balanced between the pressures from within and without, he feels more threatened by analysis than the adult, and his defenses are kept up more rigidly.[4] This refers to the whole of childhood but is felt with special intensity at the beginning of adolescence. To ward off the oncoming adolescent increase in drive activity, the adolescent normally strengthens his defenses and, with it, his resistance to analysis.

(v) Since during the entire course of childhood the most primitive methods of defense continue to operate alongside the more mature ones, the ego

[3] See above: action instead of free association.
[4] See above: refusal of free association.

resistances based on defenses are increased in number, compared with the adult.

(vi) Since habitually his ego sides with his resistances, every child wishes to abscond from analysis in times of heightened pressure from unconscious material or intense negative transference, and would do so if not held in treatment by the parents' support.

(vii) Since the urge to outgrow and reject the past is stronger during some periods of development than during others, the child's resistance to analysis fluctuates accordingly. An instance of the kind is the transition phase between oedipal and latency period. According to the dictates of development, the infantile past is closed off here, turned away from, and covered by amnesia; according to the dictates of analysis, communication with the past has to be kept open. Hence the clash between the two concerns. For the neurotic or otherwise disturbed child the need for therapy does not lessen at this time, but his willingness to undergo it does.

The same happens again during adolescence, when the adolescent needs to move away from his childhood objects, while analysis promotes the revival of the infantile relationships in the transference. This is felt as a special threat by the patient and frequently causes the abrupt ending of treatment.

(viii) Since all children tend to externalize their inner conflicts in the form of battles with the environment, they look for environmental solutions in preference to internal change. When this defense predominates, the child shows total unwillingness to undergo analysis, an attitude which is frequently mistaken for "negative transference" and (unsuccessfully) interpreted as such.

Altogether, the child analyst is faced by many difficult treatment situations which tax his skill. What he feels most acutely is the fact that for long stretches of the analysis he has to manage without a therapeutic alliance with his patient.

Transference

Taught by experience, by the elimination of the introductory phase (except in selected cases), and by the deliberate use of defense analysis (Bornstein, 1949) as an introduction, I have modified my former opinion that transference in childhood is restricted to single "transference reactions" and does not develop to the complete status of a "transference neurosis." Nevertheless, I am still unconvinced that what is called transference neurosis with children equals the adult variety in every respect. The question whether this is the case or not is all the more difficult to answer since it is obscured by two of the peculiarities of child analysis mentioned before: without the use of free association not all the evidence for the child's transference appears in the material; and owing to the child's acting instead of associating, the aggressive transference is overemphasized and overshadows the libidinal one.

On the side of adult treatment, the position with regard to transference has been a controversial subject in recent years. Some of us still adhere to the more orthodox belief that at the beginning of treatment a real (doctor-patient) relationship exists which gradually and increasingly becomes distorted through the addition of regressive libidinal and aggressive elements which are transferred from the past onto the person of the analyst, and that this continues until in the fully formed transference neurosis the realistic relationship is completely submerged under the irrealistic one. The former is expected to re-establish itself at the very end of treatment after the infantile elements have been detached from it by interpretation and after the transference phenomena have accomplished the task ascribed to them: to provide insight.

A more current view expects the transference manifestations to be in evidence from the outset of analysis and in need of interpretation as such, not only in comparison with the realistic attitudes which they replace. Since they are considered to be of prime importance, they crowd out most other sources of material for the analyst, and become the "royal road to the unconscious," a title of honor which, in the past, had been reserved for dreams. In extreme instances, the analyst's involvement with this aspect of the treatment can become so great that he is in danger of forgetting that transference is a means to an end, not a therapeutic measure in itself.

The latter views about transference seem to me to be based on three assumptions:

(1) that whatever happens in a patient's personality structure can be analyzed in terms of his object relationship to the analyst;

(2) that all levels of object relationship are equally open to interpretation and changed by it to the same extent;

(3) that the only function of the figures in the environment is to be the recipients of libidinal and aggressive cathexis and that there is no other.

When checking these assumptions against the experience
of the child analyst, some light may be shed in turn on
their relevance for adults.

THE CHILD ANALYST AS A NEW OBJECT

In child analysis, more than with adults, it becomes obvious
that the person of the analyst is used by the patient in a
variety of ways.

As discussed before,[5] all individuals, as they develop and
mature, have a hunger for *new experience* which is as strong
as the urge to *repeat*. The former is an important part of
the child's normal equipment; nevertheless, neurotic development tips the balance in favor of the latter. The child
who enters analysis sees in the analyst a new object and
treats him as such, so far as he has a healthy part to his personality. He uses the analyst for repetition, i.e., transference
so far as his neurosis or other disturbance comes into question. The double relationship is not easily handled by the
analyst. If he accepts the status of new object, different from
the parents, he undoubtedly interferes with the transference
reactions. If he ignores or rejects this side of the relationship, he disappoints the child patient in expectations which
the latter feels to be legitimate. He is then also apt to interpret items of behavior as transferred which, in fact, are
nothing of the kind. To learn how to sort out the mixture
and to move carefully between the two roles which are

[5] See this Chapter, The Curative Tendencies.

thrust on him are essential elements of every child analyst's training in technique.

The element of "new object," i.e., of attitudes to the analyst which are not transferred, is not absent from adult analysis and to highlight them is useful. But the hunger for new experience is in the mature individual neither as central nor as powerful as it is in the child. Where it enters into the relationship to the analyst, it usually serves the function of resistance.

THE CHILD ANALYST AS THE OBJECT OF LIBIDINAL AND
AGGRESSIVE TRANSFERENCE

As regards transference proper, in the course of analysis, children, like adults, repeat by means of regression and stage around the person of the analyst their object relations from all levels of development. Narcissism, unity with the mother, need fulfillment, object constancy, ambivalence, oral, anal, and phallic-oedipal stage, all contribute elements which enter the treatment situation at one time or another, often in reverse order, but also according to the type of disturbance, i.e., the depth of regression in which the child finds himself at the beginning of treatment. Besides supplying information which of these levels has been the most significant in the individual's pathogenesis, the various transferred trends color the analytic situation each in its own way. Narcissistic self-sufficiency appears in the form of withdrawal from the object world, including the analyst, i.e., as a barrier to analytic effort. Symbiotic attitudes reappear as the wish for complete and uninterrupted merging with the analyst; in adults this is often expressed as a pleading for hypnosis. Re-emergence of the anaclitic dependence proves to be a special difficulty in analysis. It disguises itself as the wish to be helped, but the onus for help is placed altogether on the analyst. The (child or adult) patient on his part is ready to break off the emotional tie as soon as demands for efforts and sacrifices are made on him. The return of oral attitudes supplies the demandingness of the patient toward the analyst as well as the dissatisfaction with what is offered (with the child for play material, etc., with the adult for attention); transference of anal trends introduces the stubbornness of the patient, the withholding of material, the provocations, the hostile and sadistic attacks which create difficulties for the analyst, not with the free associations of the adult but with the acting-out child patient. The need to be loved and the fear of object loss are transferred as suggestibility and compliance toward the analyst; in spite of their positive surface appearance, both are dreaded by the analyst, justifiably so since they are responsible for the misleading transference improvements. In short, pregenitality and preoedipal trends introduce into the transference relationship the whole host of negative, quasi-"resistant" elements. In contrast to this are the beneficial elements contributed by the appearance in the transference of object constancy and the attitudes belonging to the positive and negative oedipus complex with the coordinated ego achievements of self-observation, insight, and secondary process functioning. These cement the treatment alliance with the analyst and make it withstand all the ups and downs and vicissitudes of therapy.

According to the above reasoning, the preoedipal elements of the transference need to be interpreted before the oedipal ones. This, perhaps, can be taken as a variation of Freud's early technical recommendation to analyze trans-

ference at the point where it is used for purposes of resistance. It applies, of course, equally to the analyses of children
and adults.

For the child analyst, the foregoing explains some of
the technical difficulties experienced with the very young
before they have reached the phallic-oedipal level and with
those older children whose development has been arrested
(in contrast to regression) at one of the preoedipal levels.
Neither type of child can be expected to answer to a method
which is based on voluntary cooperation with the analyst,
i.e., on attitudes not yet acquired by them, and technical
alterations have to be introduced for them. Much has been
learned in this respect from the treatment of deprived,
homeless, motherless, and concentration camp children.
These patients who had never reached object constancy in
their relationships were found unable to establish firm and
enduring treatment alliances with their analysts in the transference (see Edith Ludowyk Gyomroi, 1963).

THE CHILD ANALYST AS OBJECT FOR EXTERNALIZATION

Not all the relations established or transferred by a child
in analysis are object relations in the sense that the analyst
becomes cathected with libido or aggression. Many are due
to externalizations, i.e., to processes in which the person of
the analyst is used to represent one or the other part of the
patient's personality structure.[6]

So far as the analyst "seduces" the child by tolerating
freedom of thought, fantasy, and action (the latter within
limits), he becomes the representative of the patient's *id*,

[6] See in this connection the studies of Warren M. Brodey (1964)
who states the same with regard to the child's pathological relationships within the family.

with all the positive and negative implications this has for the relationship. So far as he verbalizes and helps in the fight against anxiety, he becomes an *auxiliary ego* to whom the child clings for protection. Due to his being an adult, the analyst is seen and treated by the child also as an *external superego*, i.e., paradoxically as a moral judge of the very derivatives which have been liberated by his efforts.

The child thus re-stages his internal (intersystemic) conflicts as external battles with the analyst, a process which provides useful material. To interpret such externalizations in terms of object relationship within the transference would be a mistake, even though originally all conflicts within the structure have their source in earliest relationships. At the time of therapy, however, their importance lies in the fact that they reveal what happens in the child's inner world, in the relations between his internal agencies, as contrasted with the emotional relationships to objects in the external world.

The analyst of adults is not unfamiliar with the externalization of intersystemic as well as intrasystemic conflicts in his patients. Severe obsessional neurotics stage quarrels between themselves and their analyst about minor matters to escape from painful inward indecisions caused by ambivalence. Conflicts between active and passive, masculine and feminine strivings are externalized by attributing the wish for one of the two possible solutions to the analyst and fighting him as its representative. In the analysis of drug addicts, the analyst represents at the same time or in quick alternation either the object of the craving, i.e., the drug itself, or an auxiliary ego called upon to help in the fight against the drug. The analyst's role as auxiliary ego is well known also from the treatment of borderline schizophrenics. A confused patient, frightened by his own paranoid fantasies, will use the analyst's presence to strengthen his sanity. The tone of the analyst's voice, the wording of an interpretation (rather than its content) may make primary process thinking fade into the background. Such patients cling to the analyst as their external ego, but this is completely different from the clinging of the hysterical patient who desires his analyst as an object for his passion.

Understood in this manner, externalization is a subspecies of transference. Treated as such in interpretation and kept separate from transference proper, it is a valuable source of insight into the psychic structure.

INFANTILE DEPENDENCY AS A FACTOR IN ADULT AND CHILD ANALYSIS

Some of the most lively controversies concerning the specificity of child analysis are related to the question whether and how far parents should be included in the therapeutic process. Although this is overtly a technical point, the issue at stake is a theoretical one, namely, the decision whether and from which point onward a child should cease to be considered as a product and dependent of his family and should be given the status of a separate entity, a psychic structure in its own right.

Infantile dependency as an agent in character formation and neurogenesis is a familiar concept in Freud's writings, where it is dealt with as a "biological fact" and held responsible for almost all the personality gains of the developing human being. To the fear of object loss, of loss of love, of punishment to which the dependent child is exposed, he ascribes the latter's "educational compliance" which, in the adult, turns into fear of being disapproved of by the community, i.e., "social compliance." To the fear of conscience (guilt) as the residue and outcome of the dependent period, he ascribes the tendency to become neurotic. The long period of the human child's dependency is held responsible by him also for such vital matters as the capacity to form object relationships in general, and the oedipus complex in particular; the cultural struggle against aggression and the need for religion; in short, for the individual's humanization, socialization, and his ethical and moral needs.[7]

[7] See in this respect especially the following of S. Freud's writings:

". . . the biological facts that the young of the human race pass through a long period of dependence and are slow in reaching maturity . . ." (1919, p. 261).

". . . that the Oedipus complex is the psychical correlate of two fundamental biological facts: the long period of the human child's dependence . . ." (1924, p. 208).

"The biological factor is the long period of time during which the young of the human species is in a condition of helplessness and dependence. Its intra-uterine existence seems to be short in comparison with that of most animals, and it is sent into the world in a less finished state. As a result, the influence of the real external world upon it is intensified and an early differentiation between the ego and id is promoted. Moreover, the dangers of the external world have a greater importance for it, so that the value of the object which can alone protect it against them and take the place of its former intra-uterine life is enormously enhanced. The biological factor, then, establishes the earliest situations of danger and creates the need to be loved which will accompany the child through the rest of its life" (1926, p. 154f.).

"The defence against childish helplessness is what lends its characteristic features to the . . . formation of religion" (1927, p. 24).

The motive for the cultural struggle against aggression "is easily discovered in his [the child's] helplessness and his dependence on other people, and it can be best designated as fear of loss of love" (1930, p. 124).

Dependency as a Factor in Adult Analysis

Notwithstanding the fact that thus the importance of dependency was never in question in the case of adult patients, this referred only to their antecedents, i.e., to the genetic aspect of the matter. So far as the dynamic, topographical, and economic aspects were concerned, the patients were taken as independent beings, with inner agencies and structures of their own and with the neurotic conflict located within the personality, only secondarily touching on and connected with the environment.

What followed from this view for therapy was inescapable. The analytic technique was devised strictly for use within the structure: the material to be given by the patient himself, about himself; the environment to be seen not objectively, but subjectively through the patient's eyes; the relations between analyst and patient private and exclusive; the past and present relationships of the patient to be re-enacted in this privacy.

In spite of some dissenting opinions,[8] this remained the framework within which the technique for the analysis of adults developed further.

Dependency as a Factor in Child Analysis

Obviously, none of this is of help to the child analyst, who meets dependency while it is an ongoing process. It is left to him to assess the range of its present influence on his patient so far as developmental status, pathogenesis, and therapy are concerned.

[8] See, for example, R. Laforgue's (1936) statements on family neurosis and need for treatment of several family members.

As regards the patient's developmental status, i.e., the steps taken by him toward attaining individuality, it is essential for the analyst to realize in which of the vital respects the child leans on the parents and how far he has outgrown them. Whether the *state of his dependency*, or independence, is in accordance with his chronological age can be assessed approximately from the following uses a child makes consecutively of the parents:

for narcissistic unity with a motherly figure, at the age when no distinction is made between self and environment;

for leaning on their capacity to understand and manipulate external conditions so that body needs and drive derivatives can be satisfied;

as figures in the external world to whom initially narcissistic libido can be attached and where it can be converted into object libido;

to act as limiting agents to drive satisfaction, thereby initiating the child's own ego mastery of the id;

to provide the patterns for identification which are needed for building up an independent structure.

As regards the parents' role in the *causation of illness*, the child analyst has to exercise great care so as not to be misled by surface appearances and, above all, not to confuse the effect of a child's abnormality on the mother with the mother's pathogenic influence on the child.[9] The safest and most painstaking method for assessing the interaction is the simultaneous analysis of parents and their

[9] As is done easily, especially with autistic children.

children.[10] From these analyses a number of findings emerge concerning pathogenic parent-child relations such as the following:

There are parents whose attachment to the child depends on the latter's representing for them either an ideal of themselves or a figure of their own past. To retain parental love under these conditions, the child allows his personality to be molded into a pattern which is not his own and which conflicts with or neglects his own innate potentialities.

Some mothers, or fathers, assign to the child a role in their own pathology and relate to the child on this basis, not on the basis of the child's real needs.

Many mothers actually pass on their symptoms to their young children and subsequently act them out together with them in the form of a *folie à deux* (see Dorothy Burlingham et al., 1955).

In all instances mentioned, the pathological consequences for the child are all the more intense, the more the parent expresses his abnormal relationship in action as distinct from fantasies. Where the former happens, it is actually only the parent's own or simultaneous treatment which sufficiently loosens the bond between the partners to act as a therapeutic measure for the child.[11]

Parents may also play a part in *maintaining* a child's disturbance. Some of the phobias of childhood, food avoidances, sleeping rituals are kept up by the child patient only in collusion with the mother. Owing to her dreading the

[10] As it is being carried out in the Hampstead Child-Therapy Clinic as well as in other places.

[11] See, in this connection, Dorothy Burlingham et al. (1955); Ilse Hellmann et al. (1960); Kata Levy (1960); Marjorie Sprince (1962).

child's anxiety attacks as much as the child does himself, the mother participates actively in keeping up defenses, precautions, etc., and thereby camouflages the extent of the child's illness.[12] Some symptomatic, especially obsessional, actions are actually carried out on the mother's instead of on the child's own body. Some parents, for pathological reasons of their own, seem to need an ill, disturbed, or infantile child and maintain the status quo for that purpose.

As regards the carrying out of *therapy*, the analyst of children has every reason to envy his colleagues who deal with their adult patients in a person-to-person relationship. In child analysis, it is not the patient's ego but the parents' reason and insight on which beginning, continuance, and completion of treatment must rely. It is the task of the parents to help the child's ego to overcome resistances and periods of negative transference without truanting from analysis. The analyst is helpless if they fall down on this task and side with the child's resistances instead. In periods of positive transference the parents often aggravate the loyalty conflict between analyst and parent which invariably arises in the child.

The child analysts' techniques of dealing with the parents vary widely from the extreme at one end of excluding them from the intimacy of the treatment altogether, to keeping them informed, permitting them to participate in sessions (with the very young), treating or analyzing them simultaneously but separately, to the opposite extreme of treating them for the child's disturbance in preference to analyzing the child himself.

[12] See the experiences in the last war when many neurotic disturbances came into the open (as distinct from being produced) after children were separated from their homes.

Recent Studies of Dependency

Two recent papers on the theory of the parent-infant relationship have summarized the analyst's position to date, Phyllis Greenacre (1960) centering the material around the process of *maturation*, Winnicott (1960) around the facts and consequences of *maternal care*. Together, these papers present a comprehensive picture of the events of the preverbal phase of complete dependency, of the internal and external influences at work in it, and of the role played by them in shaping future normality and abnormality.

There are many other analytic studies, derived from work inside and outside the analytic session, each concentrating on a different aspect of the topic, such as: empathy between mother and child during complete dependency (Winnicott, 1949); the contribution of the phase of dependency to the constitution of the individual (Martin James, 1960); harmful consequences of disregarding and interrupting the state of dependency (A. Freud and D. Burlingham, 1943, 1944; John Bowlby et al., 1952; James Robertson, 1958; R. Spitz, 1945, 1946); the far-reaching influence of the mother's preferences and attitudes during the period of complete dependency (Joyce Robertson, 1962).

THE BALANCE BETWEEN INTERNAL AND EXTERNAL FORCES AS SEEN BY CHILD AND ADULT ANALYST

Constant contact with the child's emotional dependency on the parents has far-reaching consequences for the theoretical outlook of the child analyst.

The analyst of adults, due to the impressions which he

receives in his daily work, is in no danger of becoming an environmentalist. The power of mind over matter, i.e., of the internal over the external world, is presented to him in an unending series of examples by his patients: in the changing aspect of the circumstances of their real life which is brought about by their mood swings from elation to depression; in the use made by them of elements in the environment to fit and feed unconscious fantasies; in their projections which turn harmless, indifferent, or benevolent fellow beings into persecutors; in the distortion of the analyst's own image which serves an irrational and at times delusional (Little, 1958) transference, etc. It is especially the latter which accounts for the analyst's readiness to believe that also in the patient's childhood similar forces were at work, and that internal, not external factors, are responsible for the causation of his illness.

In short, the analyst of adults is a firm believer in psychic, as opposed to external, reality. If anything, he is too eager to see during his therapeutic work all current happenings in terms of resistance and of transference, and thereby to discount their value in reality.

For the analyst of children, on the other hand, all the indications point in the opposite direction, bearing witness to the powerful influence of the environment. In treatment, especially the very young reveal the extent to which they are dominated by the object world, i.e., how much of their behavior and pathology is determined by environmental influences such as the parents' protective or rejecting, loving or indifferent, critical or admiring attitudes, as well as by the sexual harmony or disharmony in their married life. The child's symbolic play in the analytic session communicates not only his internal fantasies; simultaneously it is his manner of communicating current family events, such as nightly intercourse between the parents, their marital quarrels and upsets, their frustrating and anxiety-arousing actions, their abnormalities and pathological expressions. The child analyst who interprets exclusively in terms of the inner world is in danger of missing out on his patient's reporting activity concerning his—at the time equally important—environmental circumstances.[13]

But in spite of accumulated evidence that adverse environmental circumstances have pathological results, nothing should convince the child analyst that alterations in external reality can work cures, except perhaps in earliest infancy. Such a belief would imply that external factors alone can be pathogenic agents and that their interaction with internal ones can be taken lightly. Such an assumption runs counter to the experience of the analyst. Every psychoanalytic investigation shows that pathogenic factors are operative on both sides, and once they are intertwined, pathology becomes ingrained in the structure of the personality and is removed only by therapeutic measures which effect the structure.

While the analysts of adults have to remind themselves of the frustrating, external, precipitating causes of the disorder of their patients, so as not to be blinded by the powers

[13] His "testificatory gestures," according to a term introduced by Augusta Bonnard.

Also in the analyses of older children where words take the place of symbolic play, current external events often dominate the material in the place of internal matters. But this use of external reality is mostly defensive and serves the purpose of the manifold resistances.

of the inner world, the child analysts have to remember that the detrimental external factors which crowd their view achieve their pathological significance by way of inter-action with the innate disposition and acquired, internal-ized libidinal and ego attitudes.

Together the two procedures, adult and child analysis, may help to maintain the balanced outlook demanded by Freud's etiological formula of a sliding scale of internal and external influences: that there are people whose "sex-ual constitution would not have led them into a neurosis if they had not had . . . [certain] experiences, and these experiences would not have had a traumatic effect on them if their libido had been otherwise disposed" (S. Freud, 1916-1917, p. 347).

In spite of their theoretical convictions, child analysts are tempted over and over again to explore the scope within which the etiological equation operates, i.e., to probe whether there are any quantitative limits beyond which the pathogenic influences can be seen as unilateral. Such re-searches can be carried out by selecting for child analysis patients from the two extreme ends of the etiological scale, i.e., those where either the innate or the environmental damage is of a massive nature. Cases of the first kind are individuals with major inborn contraindications for normal development such as severe sensory or physical handicaps (blindness, deafness, deformities, etc.); cases of the latter kind are severely traumatized children, children of psy-chotic parents, orphaned, institutional children, i.e., those where the outward setting for the normal childhood com-plexes is missing. But so far, the material gained from the treatment of such cases also shows no clinical picture de-termined by only one set of factors. Although certain pathological formations are inevitable when the pathogenic influences on either the internal or external side reach this magnitude, their range and the detailed characteristics of the personalities of the children depend, as in the less severe cases, on the interaction between the two sides, i.e., on the manner in which a particular constitution reacts to a particular set of external circumstances.

CHAPTER 3

The Assessment of Normality in Childhood

I

EARLY SPOTTING OF PATHOGENIC AGENTS; PREVENTION AND PREDICTION

It is one thing for the child analyst to reconstruct a patient's past or trace back symptoms to their origins in earliest years, and quite a different one to spot pathogenic agents before they have done their work; to assess the degree of a young child's normal progress; to predict developments; to interfere with the child's management; to guide his parents; or, in general, to work for the prevention of neuroses, psychoses, and dissociality. While the recognized training for psychoanalytic therapy will prepare the child analyst for the former tasks, no official curriculum has been devised so far to equip him for the latter.

Concern with problems such as prediction or prevention leads inevitably to a study of the normal, as opposed to the study of the pathological mental processes, or the sliding transitions between the two states with which the analyst of adults is concerned. This knowledge of the normal, still called an "underdeveloped" or "distressed" area of psycho-analysis by Ernst Kris in 1951, has been increased considerably in recent years, thanks mainly to the theoretical extrapolations from clinical findings made by Heinz Hartmann and Ernst Kris. It owes a great deal also to the increasing importance played in metapsychological thinking by the principles and assumptions of psychoanalytic child psychology, which "embraces the total field of normal and abnormal development" (Ernst Kris, 1951, p. 15). The analyst of adults has little concern in his clinical work with the concept of normality, except marginally, where functioning (in love, sex, and successful work) is concerned. In contrast, the child analyst, who sees progressive development as the most essential function of the immature, is deeply and centrally involved with the intactness or disturbance, i.e., the normality or abnormality of this vital process.

As I have set out on a former occasion (1945), development can be assessed and indications for a child's need for treatment can be gathered through scrutinizing on the one hand the libidinal and aggressive, on the other the ego and superego sides of a child's personality for signs of age-adequateness, precocity, or retardation. With the sequence of libidinal phases and a list of ego functions in the background of his mind, this is not an impossible task for the child analyst, nor even a difficult one. But the indications which emerge are more useful for the diagnosis of pathology and a revelation of the past than they are for deciding issues which concern the normal or the outlook for the future. They demonstrate in a fairly satisfactory way the compromise formations and solutions which have been achieved in the patient's personality; but they do not include signs of what the chances are of maintaining, improving, or lowering his performance level.

THE TRANSLATION OF EXTERNAL EVENTS INTO INTERNAL EXPERIENCE

Analysts, so far as they are regarded as child experts, are confronted by the public with a multitude of questions as they arise normally during the upbringing of any child and concern all the decisions about the child's life which can become problematic to the parents. That they refer to everyday situations is no reason why the answers to them should be left to the analytically untaught, who deal habitually with normal mental life (such as the parents themselves, pediatricians, nurses, nursery school teachers, teachers, welfare workers, school officers, etc.). In fact, the questions which are raised circumscribe the very areas within which the psychoanalytic theories can be applied profitably to preventive work. The following are some examples:

Should the mother of a young infant have his sole care, and does the introduction of any kind of mother substitute imply a threat to his development? Where she has sole care, when can she be permitted for the first time to leave the infant for a short spell for the benefit of a holiday, for her husband, older children, her own parents, etc.? What are the advantages of breast feeding versus bottle feeding, or of feeding by demand versus feeding by the clock? What is the best age for beginning toilet training? At what age do children actually benefit from the inclusion of other adults or of playmates? What is the right age for entry into nursery school? If surgery has to be performed (for necessary repairs, for circumcision, tonsillectomy, etc.) and if there is a choice of date, is it better to let this happen earlier or later? What type of schooling (formal or informal) is suited best to which type of child? When should sexual enlightenment be introduced? Are there any ages when the arrival of a sibling will be more easily tolerated than at other times? What about the autoerotic activities? Should sucking, masturbation, etc., be permitted without checking, and should the same apply to sex play among the children? What about the freedom of aggression? When and in what way should an adopted child be told about adoption, and does information about the natural parents have to be included? What are the pros and cons concerning day or boarding school? And finally: is there a specific moment during the adolescent process when it is helpful for the young person to "remove" (Anny Katan, 1937) himself bodily from home in addition to his emotional estrangement from his parents?

When faced with any, even the apparently simplest of these questions, the analyst's reaction has to be a double one. It is obviously not enough for him to point out that there are no general answers which fit all children, only particular ones to fit a given child; to warn against basing solutions on chronological age, since children differ as much in the rate of their emotional and social growth as they differ in their physical milestones and their mental ages; or even to assess the developmental level of the child on whose behalf he is consulted. Considerations of this kind constitute only one part of his assignment, and perhaps the easier one. The other and no less essential half consists of assessing the psychological meaning of the experience or demand to which the parents intend to subject the child. While the parents may view their plans in the light of reason, logic, and practical necessity, the child experiences them in terms of his psychic reality, i.e., according to the phase-adequate complexes, affects, anxieties, and fantasies which are aroused by them. It therefore becomes the analyst's task to point out to the parents the discrepancies which exist between the adult's and the child's interpretation of events and to explain the latter on the basis of the specific modes and levels of functioning which are characteristic of the infantile mind.

FOUR AREAS OF DIFFERENCE BETWEEN CHILD AND ADULT

There are several areas in the child's mind from which such "misunderstandings" of adult actions are known to arise.

There is, for one, the *egocentricity* which governs the infant's relations with the object world. Before the phase of object constancy has been reached, the object, i.e., the mothering person, is not perceived by the child as having an existence of her own; she is perceived only in terms of a role assigned to her within the framework of the child's needs and wishes. Accordingly, whatever happens in or to the object is understood from the aspect of satisfaction or frustration of these wishes. Every preoccupation of the mother, her concerns with other members of the family, with work or outside interests, her depressions, illnesses, absences, even her death, are transformed thereby into experiences of rejection and desertion. On the same basis the birth of a sibling is understood as unfaithfulness of the parents, as dissatisfaction with and criticism of the child's own person—in short, as a hostile act to which the child in his turn answers with hostility and disappointment expressed either in excessive demandingness or in emotional withdrawal with its adverse consequences.

There is, secondly, the very *immaturity* of the infantile *sexual apparatus* which leaves the child no choice but to translate adult genital happenings into pregenital events. This accounts for parental intercourse being misunderstood as a scene of brutal violence and opens the door for all the difficulties of identifying with either the alleged victim or alleged aggressor which reveal themselves later in the growing child's uncertainty about his own sexual identity. It also accounts, as has been well known for a considerable period, for the comparative failure and parental disappointments in sexual enlightenment. Instead of accepting the sexual facts as reasonably as they are given, the child cannot help but translate them into the terms which are commensurate with his experience, i.e., turn them into the so-called "infantile sexual theories" of impregnation through the mouth (as in fairy tales), birth through the anus, castration of the female partner through intercourse, etc.

Thirdly, there are those occasions where the child's misapprehension of events is based not on an absolute lack of reasoning on his part but on economic factors, i.e., on the *relative weakness of secondary process* thinking compared with the strength of impulses and fantasies. A young child after the toddler stage, for example, may be well able to grasp the significance of medical events, to recognize the role of doctor or surgeon as a beneficient one, the necessity for medicines whatever their taste, the need for dietary ' or motor restrictions, etc. Only this understanding cannot be expected to maintain itself. As the visit to the doctor or an impending operation come nearer, reason goes by the board and the child's mind is swamped by fantasies of mutilation, castration, violent assault, etc. Being kept in bed becomes imprisonment; the diet is felt as intolerable oral deprivation; the parents who permit these things to happen to the child (in their presence or absence) cease to be protective figures and are turned into hostile ones against whom the child's own anger, rage, hostility can be released.[1]

Finally, there are some basic differences between the functioning of the child's mind and that of the adult and these are significant in this respect. I mention as their most important representative the different *evaluation of time* at the various age levels. The sense of the length or shortness of a given time period seems to depend on the measuring being carried out by way of either id or ego functioning. Id impulses are by definition intolerant of delay and waiting; the latter attitudes are introduced by the ego of which postponement of action (by interpolation of the thought processes) is as characteristic as urgency of fulfillment is of the id. How a child will experience a given time period will depend therefore not on the actual duration, measured objectively by the adult, by the calendar and by the clock, but on the subjective inner relations of either id or ego dominance over his functioning. It is these latter factors which will decide whether the intervals set for feeding, the absence of the mother, the duration of nursery attendance,

[1] See in this respect also Anna Freud (1952), Joyce Robertson (1956).

of hospitalization, etc., will seem to the child short or long, tolerable or intolerable, and as a result will prove harmless or harmful in their consequences.

The child's egocentricity, the immaturity of his sex life, the preponderance of id derivatives over ego responses, his different evaluation of time are characteristics of the infantile mind which may account for many of the parents' apparent insensibilities, i.e., for their difficulty in translating external occurrences into internal experience. Information about a child's history at the diagnostic stage is therefore given by them in a cursory and misleading manner. Reports may contain an account of "a battle about breast feeding which was soon terminated"; a toddler's "initial refusal to accept a mother substitute during the mother's illness"; a boy's "turning his back on the mother momentarily when she returned from the maternity hospital with the new baby"; a child's "passing unhappiness in the hospital," etc.[2]

It requires all of the ingenuity of the diagnostician, and sometimes a period of analytic treatment, to reconstruct from descriptions of this kind the dynamic struggles which lie behind the surface picture and which, more often than not, have been responsible for changing the whole course of the child's emotional life from attachment to the parents to withdrawal from them, from love and good-will to resentment and hostility, from the feeling of being cherished to a feeling of rejection and worthlessness, etc.

---

[2] Examples quoted from the Diagnostic Service of the Hampstead Child-Therapy Clinic.

II

THE CONCEPT OF DEVELOPMENTAL LINES

For useful answers to the parents' questions concerning developmental issues, the external decisions under consideration need thus to be translated into their internal implications. As mentioned above, this cannot be done if drive and ego development are viewed in isolation from each other, necessary as this is for purposes of clinical analysis and theoretical dissection.

So far, in our psychoanalytic theory, the developmental sequences are laid down only with regard to particular, circumscribed parts of the child's personality. Concerning the development of the sexual drive, for example, we possess the sequence of libidinal phases (oral, anal, phallic, latency period, preadolescence, adolescent genitality) which, in spite of considerable overlapping, correspond roughly with specific ages. With regard to the aggressive drive we are already less precise and are usually content to correlate specific aggressive expressions with specific libidinal phases (such as biting, spitting, devouring with orality; sadistic torturing, hitting, kicking, destroying with anality; overbearing, domineering, forceful behavior with the phallic phase; inconsiderateness, mental cruelty, dissocial outbursts with adolescence, etc.). On the side of the ego, the analytically known stages and levels of the sense of reality, in the chronology of defense activity and in the growth of a moral sense, lay down a norm. The intellectual functions themselves are measured and graded by the psychologist by means of the age-related scales of the various intelligence tests.

Without doubt we need more for our assessments than these selected developmental scales which are valid for isolated parts of the child's personality only, not for its totality. What we are looking for are the basic interactions between id and ego and their various developmental levels, and also age-related sequences of them which, in importance, frequency, and regularity, are comparable to the maturational sequence of libidinal stages or the gradual unfolding of the ego functions. Naturally, such sequences of interaction between the two sides of the personality can be best established where both are well studied, as they are, for example, with regard to the libidinal phases and aggressive expressions on the id side and the corresponding object-related attitudes on the ego side. Here we can trace the combinations which lead from the infant's complete emotional dependence to the adult's comparative self-reliance and mature sex and object relationships, a gradated developmental line which provides the indispensable basis for any assessment of emotional maturity or immaturity, normality or abnormality.

Even if perhaps less easily established, there are similar lines of development which can be shown to be valid for almost every other area of the individual's personality. In every instance they trace the child's gradual outgrowing of dependent, irrational, id- and object-determined attitudes to an increasing ego mastery of his internal and external world. Such lines—always contributed to from the side of both id and ego development—lead, for example, from the infant's suckling and weaning experiences to the adult's rational rather than emotional attitude to food intake; from cleanliness training enforced on the child by environmental pressure to the adult's more or less ingrained and unshakable bladder and bowel control; from the child's sharing possession of his body with his mother to the adolescent's claim for independence and self-determination in body management; from the young child's egocentric view of the world and his fellow beings to empathy, mutuality, and companionship with his contemporaries; from the first erotic play on his own and his mother's body by way of the transitional objects (Winnicott, 1953) to the toys, games, hobbies, and finally to work, etc.

Whatever level has been reached by any given child in any of these respects represents the results of interaction between drive and ego-superego development and their reaction to environmental influences, i.e., between maturation, adaptation, and structuralization. Far from being theoretical abstractions, developmental lines, in the sense here used, are historical realities which, when assembled, convey a convincing picture of an individual child's personal achievements or, on the other hand, of his failures in personality development.

Prototype of a Developmental Line: From Dependency to Emotional Self-Reliance and Adult Object Relationships

To serve as the prototype for all others, there is one basic developmental line which has received attention from analysts from the beginning. This is the sequence which leads from the newborn's utter dependence on maternal care to the young adult's emotional and material self-reliance—a sequence for which the successive stages of libido development (oral, anal, phallic) merely form the inborn, maturational base. The steps on this way are well documented from the analyses of adults and children, as well as from direct analytic infant observations. They can be listed, roughly, as follows:

(1)   The biological unity between the mother-infant couple, with the mother's narcissism extending to the child, and the child including the mother in his internal "narcissistic milieu" (Hoffer, 1952), the whole period being further subdivided (according to Margaret Mahler, 1952) into the autistic, symbiotic, and separation-individuation phases with significant danger points for developmental disturbances lodged in each individual phase;

(2)   the part object (Melanie Klein), or need-fulfilling, anaclitic relationship, which is based on the urgency of the child's body needs and drive derivatives and is intermittent and fluctuating, since object cathexis is sent out under the impact of imperative desires, and withdrawn again when satisfaction has been reached;

(3)   the stage of object constancy, which enables a positive inner image of the object to be maintained, irrespective of either satisfactions or dissatisfactions;

(4)   the ambivalent relationship of the preoedipal, anal-sadistic stage, characterized by the ego attitudes of clinging, torturing, dominating, and controlling the love objects;

(5)   the completely object-centered phallic-oedipal phase, characterized by possessiveness of the parent of the opposite sex (or vice versa), jealousy of and rivalry with the parent of the same sex, protectiveness, curiosity, bids

for admiration, and exhibitionistic attitudes; in girls a phallic-oedipal (masculine) relationship to the mother preceding the oedipal relationship to the father;

(6) the latency period, i.e., the postoedipal lessening of drive urgency and the transfer of libido from the parental figures to contemporaries, community groups, teachers, leaders, impersonal ideals, and aim-inhibited, sublimated interests, with fantasy manifestations giving evidence of disillusionment with and denigration of the parents ("family romance," twin fantasies, etc.);

(7) the preadolescent prelude to the "adolescent revolt," i.e., a return to early attitudes and behavior, especially of the part-object, need-fulfilling, and ambivalent type;

(8) the adolescent struggle around denying, reversing, loosening, and shedding the tie to the infantile objects, defending against pregenitality, and finally establishing genital supremacy with libidinal cathexis transferred to objects of the opposite sex, outside the family.

While the details of these positions have long been common knowledge in analytic circles, their relevance for practical problems is being explored increasingly in recent years. As regards, for example, the much-discussed consequences of a child's separation from the mother, the parents or the home, a mere glance at the unfolding of the developmental line will be sufficient to show convincingly why the common reactions to, respectively, the pathological consequences of, such happenings are as varied as they are, following the varying psychic reality of the child on the different levels. Infringements of the biological mother-infant tie (phase 1), for whatever reason they are undertaken, will thus give rise to separation anxiety (Bowlby, 1960) proper; failure of the mother to play her part as a reliable need-fulfilling and comfort-giving agency (phase 2) will cause breakdowns in individuation (Mahler, 1952) or anaclitic depression (Spitz, 1946), or other manifestations of deprivation (Alpert, 1959), or precocious ego development (James, 1960), or what has been called a "false self" (Winnicott, 1955). Unsatisfactory libidinal relations to unstable or otherwise unsuitable love objects during anal sadism (phase 4) will disturb the balanced fusion between libido and aggression and give rise to uncontrollable aggressivity, destructiveness, etc. (A. Freud, 1949). It is only after object constancy (phase 3) has been reached that the external absence of the object is substituted for, at least in part, by the presence of an internal image which remains stable; on the strength of this achievement temporary separations can be lengthened, commensurate with the advances in object constancy. Thus, even if it remains impossible to name the chronological age when separations can be tolerated, according to the developmental line it can be stated when they become phase-adequate and nontraumatic, a point of practical importance for the purposes of holidays for the parents, hospitalization of the child, convalescence, entry into nursery school, etc.[3]

There are other practical lessons which have been learned from the same developmental sequence, such as the following:

that the clinging attitudes of the toddler stage (phase 4) are the result of preoedipal ambivalence, not of maternal spoiling;

[3] If, by "mourning" we understand not the various manifestations of anxiety, distress, and malfunction which accompany object loss in the earliest phases but the painful, gradual process of detaching libido from an internal image, this, of course, cannot be expected to occur before object constancy (phase 3) has been established.

that it is unrealistic on the part of parents to expect of the preoedipal period (up to the end of phase 4) the mutuality in object relations which belongs to the next level (phase 5) only;

that no child can be fully integrated in group life before libido has been transferred from the parents to the community (phase 6). Where the passing of the oedipus complex is delayed and phase 5 is protracted as the result of an infantile neurosis, disturbances in adaptation to the group, lack of interest, school phobias (in day school), extreme homesickness (in boarding school) will be the order of the day;

that reactions to adoption are most severe in the later part of the latency period (phase 6) when, according to the normal disillusionment with the parents, all children feel as if adopted and the feelings about the reality of adoption merge with the occurrence of the "family romance";

that sublimations, foreshadowed on the oedipal level (phase 5) and developed during latency (phase 6), may be lost during preadolescence (phase 7), not through any developmental or educational failure, but owing to the phase-adequate regression to early levels (phases 2, 3, and 4);

that it is as unrealistic on the part of the parents to oppose the loosening of the tie to the family or the young person's battle against pregenital impulses in adolescence (phase 8) as it is to break the biological tie in phase 1, or oppose pregenital autoerotism in the phases 1, 2, 3, 4, and 7.

Some Developmental Lines toward Body Independence

That the ego of an individual begins first and foremost as a body ego does not imply that bodily independence of the parents is reached earlier than emotional or moral self-reliance. On the contrary: the mother's narcissistic possessiveness of her infant's body is matched from the child's side by his archaic wishes to merge with the mother and by the confusion concerning body limits which arises from the fact that in early life the distinctions between the internal and external world are based not on objective reality but on the subjective experiences of pleasure and unpleasure. Thus, while the mother's breast, or face, hands, or hair, may be treated (or maltreated) by the infant as parts of his own organization, his hunger, his tiredness, his discomforts are her concern as much as they are his own. Although for the whole of early childhood the child's life will be dominated by body needs, body impulses, and their derivatives, the quantities and qualities of satisfactions and dissatisfactions are determined not by himself but by environmental influence. The only exceptions to this rule are the autoerotic gratifications which from the beginning are under the child's own management and, therefore, provide for him a certain circumscribed measure of independence of the object world. In contrast to these, as will be shown below, the processes of feeding, sleeping, evacuation, body hygiene, and prevention of injury and illness have to undergo complex and lengthy developments before they become the growing individual's own concern.

FROM SUCKLING TO RATIONAL EATING

A long line has to be passed through before a child arrives at the point where, for example, he can regulate his own food intake actively and rationally, quantitatively and qualitatively, on the basis of his own needs and appetites and irrespective of his relations to the provider of food, and of conscious and unconscious fantasies. The steps on the way are approximately as follows:

(1) Being nursed at the breast or bottle, by the clock or on demand, with the common difficulties about intake caused partly by the infant's normal fluctuations of appetite and intestinal upsets, partly by the mother's attitudes and anxieties regarding feeding; interference with need satisfaction caused by hunger periods, undue waiting for meals, rationing or forced feeding set up the first—and often lasting—disturbances in the positive relationship to food. Pleasure sucking appears as a forerunner, by-product of, substitute for, or interference with feeding;

(2) weaning from breast or bottle, initiated either by the infant himself or according to the mother's wishes. In the latter instance, and especially if carried out abruptly, the infant's protest against oral deprivation has adverse results for the normal pleasure in food. Difficulties may occur over the introduction of solids, new tastes and consistencies being either welcomed or rejected;

(3) the transition from being fed to self-feeding, with or without implements, "food" and "mother" still being identified with each other;

(4) self-feeding with the use of spoon, fork, etc., the disagreements with the mother about the quantity of intake being shifted often to the form of intake, i.e., table manners; meals as a general battleground on which the difficulties of the mother-child relationship can be fought out; craving for sweets as a phase-ade-

quate substitute for oral sucking pleasures; food fads
as a result of anal training, i.e., of the newly acquired
reaction formation of disgust;

(5) gradual fading out of the equation food-mother in the
oedipal period. Irrational attitudes toward eating are
now determined by infantile sexual theories, i.e., fantasies of impregnation through the mouth (fear of
poison), pregnancy (fear of getting fat), anal birth
(fear of intake and output), as well as by reaction
formations against cannibalism and sadism;

(6) gradual fading out of the sexualization of eating in the
latency period, with pleasure in eating retained or even
increased. Increase in the rational attitudes to food
and self-determination in eating, the earlier experiences on this line being decisive in shaping the individual's food habits in adult life, his tastes, preferences,
as well as eventual addictions or aversions with regard
to food and drink.

The infant's reactions to the changes in phase 2 (i.e., to
weaning and to the introduction of new tastes and consistencies) reflect for the first time his leaning toward either
progression and adventurousness (when new experiences
are welcomed) or a tenacious clinging to existing pleasures
(when every change is experienced as threat and deprivation). It is to be expected that, whichever attitude dominates the feeding process will also become important in
other developmental areas.

The equation food-mother, which persists through phases
1-4, provides the rational background for the mother's subjective conviction that every food refusal of the child is
aimed at her personally, i.e., expresses the child's rejection

of her maternal care and attention, a conviction which causes much oversensitiveness in handling the feeding process and underlies the battle about food on the mother's side. It explains also why in these phases food refusal and extreme food fads can be circumvented by temporarily substituting a stranger, i.e., a noncathected or differently cathected person, for the maternal figure in the feeding situation. Children will then eat, in hospital, in nursery school, or as visitors, but this will not cure their eating difficulties at home, in the presence of the mother. It explains also why traumatic separations from the mother are often followed by refusal of food (rejection of the mother substitute), or by greed and overeating (treating food as a substitute for mother love).

The eating disturbances of phase 5, which are not related to an external object but are caused by internal, structural conflicts, are not affected by either the material presence or the material absence of the mother, a fact which can be utilized for differential diagnosis.

After phase 6, when the arrangements for food intake have become the mature individual's personal concern, the former food battle with the mother may be replaced by internal disagreements between the manifest wish to eat and an unconsciously determined inability to tolerate certain foods, i.e., the various neurotic food fads and digestive upsets.

FROM WETTING AND SOILING TO BLADDER AND BOWEL CONTROL

Since the desired aim on this line is not the comparatively intact survival of drive derivatives but the control, modification, and transformation of the urethral and anal trends, the conflicts between id, ego, superego, and environmental forces become particularly obvious.

(1) The duration of the first phase, during which the infant has complete freedom to wet and soil, is determined not maturationally but environmentally, i.e., by the mother's timing of her interference, in which she in her turn is under the influence of personal needs, familial, social, or medical conventions. Under present conditions this phase may last from a few days (training from birth based on reflex action) to two or three years (training based on object relatedness and ego control).

(2) In contrast to phase one, the second phase is initiated by a step in maturation. The dominant role in drive activity passes from the oral to the anal zone, and due to this transition the child stiffens his opposition to any interference with concerns which have become emotionally vital to him. Since in this phase the body products are highly cathected with libido, they are precious to the child and are treated as "gifts" which are surrendered to the mother as a sign of love; since they are cathected also with aggression, they are weapons by means of which rage, anger, disappointment can be discharged within the object relationship. In correspondence to this double cathexis of the body products, the toddler's entire attitude toward the object world is dominated by ambivalence, i.e., by violent swings between love and hate (libido and aggression not fused with each other). This again is matched on the ego side by curiosity directed toward the inside of the body, pleasure in messing, molding, play with retaining, emptying, hoarding, as well as dominating, possessing, destroying, etc. While the trends shown by the children in this phase are fairly uniform, the actual events vary with the differences in the

mother's attitude. If she succeeds in remaining sensitive to the child's needs and as identified with them as she is usually with regard to feeding, she will mediate sympathetically between the environmental demand for cleanliness and the child's opposite anal and urethral tendencies; in that case toilet training will proceed gradually, uneventfully, and without upheavals. On the other hand, such empathy with the child in the anal stage may be impossible for the mother due to her own training, her own reaction formations of disgust, orderliness, and punctiliousness, or other obsessional elements in her personality. If she is dominated by these, she will represent the demand for urethral and anal control in a harsh and uncompromising manner and a major battle will ensue, with the child as intent to defend his right over unrestricted evacuation as the mother is on achieving cleanliness and regularity and with them the rudiments and *sine qua non* of socialization.

(3) In a third phase the child accepts and takes over the mother's and the environment's attitudes to cleanliness and, through identification, makes them an integral part of his ego and superego demands; from then onward, the striving for cleanliness is an internal, not an external, precept, and inner barriers against urethral and anal wishes are set up through the defense activity of the ego, in the well-known form of repression and reaction formation. Disgust, orderliness, tidiness, dislike of dirty hands guard against the return of the repressed; punctuality, conscientiousness, and reliability appear as by-products of anal regularity; inclinations to save, to collect, give evidence of high anal evaluation displaced to other matters. In short, what takes place in this period is the far-reaching modification and transformation of the pregenital anal drive derivatives which—

if kept within normal limits—supply the individual personality with a backbone of highly valuable qualities.

It is important to remember in respect to these achievements that they are based on identifications and internalizations and, as such, are not fully secure before the passing of the oedipus complex. Preoedipal anal control remains vulnerable and, especially in the beginning of the third phase, remains dependent on the objects and the stability of positive relations to them. For example, a child who is trained to use the chamberpot or toilet in his home does not exchange them automatically for unfamiliar ones, away from the mother. A child who is severely disappointed in his mother, or separated from her, or suffering from object loss in any form, may not only lose the internalized urge to be clean but also reactivate the aggressive use of elimination. Both together will result in incidents of wetting and soiling which appear as "accidents."

(4) It is only in a fourth phase that bladder and bowel control become wholly secure. This is brought about when the concern for cleanliness is disconnected from object ties and attains the status of a fully neutralized, autonomous ego and superego concern.[4]

FROM IRRESPONSIBILITY TO RESPONSIBILITY IN
BODY MANAGEMENT

That the satisfaction of such essential physical needs as feeding and evacuation[5] remains for years under external control and emerges from it in such slow steps corresponds well with the equally slow and gradual manner in which

[4] See H. Hartmann (1950b) on "secondary autonomy of the ego."
[5] Also sleep.

children assume responsibility for the care of their own body and its protection against harm. As described at length elsewhere (A. Freud, 1952), the well-mothered child leaves these concerns largely to the mother, while he allows himself attitudes of indifference and unconcern, or, as a weapon in a battle with her, downright recklessness. It is only the badly mothered or the motherless who adopt the mother's role in health matters and play "mother and child" with their own bodies as the hypochondriacs do.

On the positive progressive line, here too, there are several consecutive phases to be distinguished from each other, though our present knowledge of them is more sketchy than in other areas.

(1) What comes first, as a maturational step in the first few months of life, is an alteration in the direction of aggression from being lived out on the body to being turned toward the external world. This vital step sets limits to self-injury from biting, scratching, etc., although indications of such tendencies can also be seen in many children as genuine remnants at later ages.[6] The normal forward move happens partly due to the setting up of the pain barrier, partly due to the child's answering to the mother's libidinal cathexis of his body with a narcissistic cathexis of his own (according to Hoffer, 1950).

(2) What makes itself felt next are the advances in ego functioning such as orientation in the external world, understanding of cause and effect, control of dangerous wishes in the service of the reality principle. Together with the

---

[6] Such remnants should not be confused with the later "turning of aggression against the self," which is not a defect in maturation but a defense mechanism used by the ego under the impact of conflict.

pain barrier and the narcissistic cathexis of the body, these newly acquired functions protect the child against such external dangers as water, fire, heights, etc. But there are many instances of children where—owing to a deficiency in any one of these ego functions—this advance is retarded so that they remain unusually vulnerable and exposed if not protected by the adult world.

(3) What comes last normally is the child's voluntary endorsement of the rules of hygiene and of medical necessities. So far as the avoidance of unwholesome food, over-eating, and keeping the body clean are concerned, this is inconclusive here since the relevant attitudes belong to the vicissitudes of the oral and anal component instinct rather than to the present line. It is different with the avoidance of ill-health or the compliance with doctor's orders concerning the intake of medicines, and motor or dietary restrictions. Fear, guilt, castration anxiety, of course, may motivate any child to be careful (i.e., fearful) for the safety of his body. But when not under the influence of these, normal children will be remarkably uncompromising and obstructive in health matters. According to their mothers' frequent complaints, they behave as if they claimed it as their right to endanger their health while they left it to their mothers to protect and restore it, an attitude which lasts often until the end of adolescence and may represent the last residue of the original symbiosis between child and mother.

Further Examples of Developmental Lines

There are many other examples of developmental lines, such as the two given below, where every step is known to the analyst, and which can be traced without difficulty, either through working backward by reconstruction from the adult picture, or through working forward by means of longitudinal analytic exploration and observation of the child.

FROM EGOCENTRICITY TO COMPANIONSHIP

When describing a child's growth in this particular respect, a sequence can be traced which runs as follows:

(1) a selfish, narcissistically orientated outlook on the object world, in which other children either do not figure at all or are perceived only in their role as disturbers of the mother-child relationship and rivals for the parents' love;   .

(2) other children related to as lifeless objects, i.e., toys which can be handled, pushed around, sought out, and discarded as the mood demands, with no positive or negative response expected from them;

(3) other children related to as helpmates in carrying out a desired task such as playing, building, destroying, causing mischief of some kind, etc., the duration of the partnership being determined by the task, and secondary to it;

(4) other children as partners and objects in their own right, whom the child can admire, fear, or compete with, whom he loves or hates, with whose feelings he identifies, whose wishes he acknowledges and often respects, and with whom he can share possessions on a basis of equality.

In the first two phases, even if cherished and tolerated as the baby by older siblings, the toddler is by necessity asocial, whatever efforts to the contrary the mother may make; community life at this stage may be endured but will not be profitable. The third stage represents the minimum requirement for socialization in the form of acceptance into a home community of older siblings or entry into a nursery group of contemporaries. But it is only the fourth stage which equips the child for companionship, enmities and friendships of any type and duration.

FROM THE BODY TO THE TOY AND FROM PLAY TO WORK

(1) Play begins with the infant as an activity yielding erotic pleasure, involving the mouth, the fingers, vision, the whole surface of the skin. It is carried out on the child's own body (autoerotic play) or on the mother's body (usually in connection with feeding) with no clear distinction between the two, and with no obvious order or precedence in this respect.

(2) The properties of the mother's and the child's body are transferred to some soft substance, such as a nappy, a pillow, a rug, a teddy, which serves as the infant's first plaything, the transitional object (according to Winnicott, 1953) which is cathected both with narcissistic and with object libido.

(3) Clinging to one specific transitional object develops further into a more indiscriminate liking for soft toys of various kinds which, as symbolic objects, are cuddled and maltreated alternately (cathected with libido and aggression). That they are inanimate objects, and therefore do not retaliate, enables the toddler to express the full range of his ambivalence toward them.

(4) Cuddly toys fade out gradually, except at bedtime,

when—in their capacity as transitional objects—they continue to facilitate the child's passing from active participation in the external world to the narcissistic withdrawal necessary for sleep.

In daytime their place is taken increasingly by play material which does not itself possess object status but which serves ego activities and the fantasies underlying them. Such activities either directly gratify a component instinct or are invested with displaced and sublimated drive energies, their chronological sequence being approximately the following:

(a) toys offering opportunities for ego activities such as filling-emptying, opening-shutting, fitting in, messing, etc., interest in them being displaced from the body openings and their functions:

(b) movable toys providing pleasure in motility;

(c) building material offering equal opportunities for construction and destruction (in correspondence with the ambivalent trends of the anal-sadistic phase);

(d) toys serving the expression of masculine and feminine trends and attitudes, to be used

    (i) in solitary role play,

    (ii) for display to the oedipal object (serving phallic exhibitionism),

    (iii) for staging the various situations of the oedipus complex in group play (provided that stage 3 on the developmental line toward companionship has been reached).

Expression of masculinity can be taken over also by the ego activities of gymnastics and acrobatics, in which the child's entire body and its skillful manipulation represent, display, and provide symbolic enjoyment from phallic activities and phallic mastery.

(5) Direct or displaced satisfaction from the play activity itself gives way increasingly to the pleasure in the finished product of the activity, a pleasure which has been described in academic psychology as pleasure in task completion, in problem solving, etc. By some authors it is taken as the indispensable prerequisite for the child's successful performance in school (Bühler, 1935).

The exact manner in which this pleasure in achievement is linked with the child's instinctual life is still an open question in our theoretical thinking, although various operative factors seem unmistakable such as imitation and identification in the early mother-child relationship, the influence of the ego ideal, the turning of passive into active as a mechanism of defense and adaptation, and the inner urge toward maturation, i.e., toward progressive development.

That pleasure in achievement, linked only secondarily with object relations, is present in very young children as a latent capacity is demonstrated in a practical manner by the successes of the Montessori method. In this nursery school method the play material is selected so as to afford the child the maximum increase in self-esteem and gratification by means of task completion and independent problem solving, and children can be observed to respond positively to such opportunities almost from the toddler stage onward.

Where this source of gratification is not tapped to the same degree with the help of external arrangements, the pleasure derived from achievement in play remains more directly connected with praise and approval given by the object world, and satisfaction from the finished product takes first place at a later date only, probably as the result of internalization of external sources of self-esteem.

(6) Ability to play changes into ability to *work*[7] when a number of additional faculties are acquired, such as the following:

(a) to control, inhibit, or modify the impulses to use given materials aggressively and destructively (not to throw, to take apart, to mess, to hoard), and to use them positively and constructively instead (to build, to plan, to learn, and—in communal life—to share);

(b) to carry out preconceived plans with a minimum regard for the lack of immediate pleasure yield, intervening frustrations, etc., and the maximum regard for the pleasure in the ultimate outcome;

(c) to achieve thereby not only the transition from primitive instinctual to sublimated pleasure, together with a high grade of neutralization of the energy employed, but equally the transition from the pleasure principle to the reality principle, a development which is essential for success in work during latency, adolescence, and in maturity.

Derived from the line from the body to the toy and from play to work and based predominantly on its later stages are a number of allied activities which are significant for personality development such as daydreaming, games, and hobbies.

---

[7] What is attempted here is not a definition of work with all its social as well as psychological implications, but merely a description of the advances in ego development and drive control which seem to be the necessary forerunners of any individual's acquisition of the capacity to work.

Daydreaming: When toys and the activities connected with them fade into the background, the wishes formerly put into action with the help of material objects, i.e., fulfilled in play, can be spun out imaginatively in the form of conscious daydreams, a fantasy activity which may persist until adolescence, and far beyond it.

Games: Games derive their origin from the imaginative group activities of the oedipal period (see stage 4, d, iii) from which they develop into the symbolic and highly formalized expression of trends toward aggressive attack, defense, competition, etc. Since they are governed by inflexible rules to which the individual participant has to submit, they cannot be entered successfully by any child before some adaptation to reality and some frustration tolerance have been acquired and, naturally, not before stage 3 on the developmental line toward companionship has been reached.

Games may require equipment (as distinct from toys). Since this is in many instances of symbolic phallic, i.e., masculine-aggressive, significance, it is highly valued by the child.

In many competitive games the child's own body and the body skills themselves play the role of indispensable tools.

Proficiency and pleasure in games are, thus, a complex achievement, dependent on contributions from many areas of the child's personality such as the endowment and intactness of the motor apparatus; a positive cathexis of the body and its skills; acceptance of companionship and group life; positive employment of controlled aggression in the service of ambition, etc. Correspondingly, functioning in this area is open to an equally large number of disturbances which may result from developmental difficulties and inadequacies in any of these areas, as well as from the phase- determined inhibitions of anal aggression and phallic-oedipal masculinity.

Hobbies: Halfway between play and work is the place of the hobbies, which have certain aspects in common with both activities. With play they share a number of characteristics:

(a) of being undertaken for purposes of pleasure with comparative disregard for external pressures and necessities;

(b) of pursuing displaced, i.e., sublimated, aims, but aims which are not too far removed from the gratification of either erotic or aggressive drives;

(c) of pursuing these aims with a combination of unmodified drive energies plus energies in various states and degrees of neutralization.

With working attitudes as described above, the hobbies share the important feature of a preconceived plan being undertaken in a reality-adapted way and carried on over a considerable period of time, if necessary in the face of external difficulties and frustrations.

Hobbies appear for the first time at the beginning of the latency period (collecting, spotting, specializing of interests), undergo any number of changes of content, but may persist as this specific form of activity throughout life.

Correspondence between Developmental Lines

If we examine our notions of average normality in detail, we find that we expect a fairly close correspondence between growth on the individual developmental lines. In clinical terms this means that, to be a harmonious personality, a child who has reached a specific stage in the sequence toward emotional maturity (for example, object constancy), should have attained also corresponding levels in his growth toward bodily independence (such as bladder and bowel control, loosening of the tie between food and mother), in the lines toward companionship, constructive play, etc. We maintain this expectation of a norm even though reality presents us with many examples to the contrary. There are numerous children, undoubtedly, who show a very irregular pattern in their growth. They may stand high on some levels (such as maturity of emotional relations, bodily independence, etc.) while lagging behind in others (such as play where they continue to cling to transitional objects, cuddly toys, or development of companionship where they persist in treating contemporaries as disturbances or inanimate objects). Some children are well developed toward secondary thought, speech, play, work, community life while remaining in a state of dependency with regard to the management of their own bodily processes, etc.

Such imbalance between developmental lines causes sufficient friction in childhood to justify a closer inquiry into the circumstances which give rise to it, especially into the question how far it is determined by innate and how far by environmental reasons.

As in all similar instances, our task is not to isolate the two factors and to ascribe to each a separate field of influence but to trace their interactions, which may be described as follows:

We assume that with all normally endowed, organically undamaged children the lines of development indicated

above are included in their constitution as inherent possibilities. What endowment lays down for them on the side
of the id are, obviously, the maturational sequences in the
development of libido and aggression; on the side of the
ego, less obviously and less well studied, certain innate tendencies toward organization, defense, and structuralization;
perhaps also, though we know less still about this, some
given quantitative differences of emphasis on progress in one
direction or another. For the rest, that is, for what singles
out individual lines for special promotion in development,
we have to look to accidental environmental influences. In
the analysis of older children and the reconstructions from
adult analysis we have found these forces embodied in the
parents' personalities, their actions and ideals, the family
atmosphere, the impact of the cultural setting as a whole.
In the analytic observation of young infants it has been
demonstrated that it is the individual mother's interest and
predilection which act as stimulants. In the beginning of
life, at least, the infant seems to concentrate on the development along those lines which call forth most ostensibly
the mother's love and approval, i.e., her spontaneous pleasure in the child's achievement and, in comparison, to neglect others where such approval is not given. This implies
that activities which are acclaimed by the mother are repeated more frequently, become libidinized, and thereby
stimulated into further growth.

For example, it seems to make a difference to the timing
of speech development and the quality of early verbalization
if a mother, for reasons of her own personality structure,
makes contact with her infant not through bodily channels
but through talking. Some mothers find no pleasure in the

growing infant's adventurousness and bodily unruliness and
have their happiest and most intimate moments when the
infant smiles. We have seen at least one such mother whose
infant made constant and inordinate use of smiling in his
approaches to the whole environment. It is not unknown
that early contact with the mother through her singing has
consequences for the later attitudes to music and may promote special musical aptitudes. On the other hand, marked
disinterest of the mother in the infant's body and his developing motility may result in clumsiness, lack of grace in
movement, etc.

It was known in psychoanalysis long before such infant
observations that depressive moods of the mother during
the first two years after birth create in the child a tendency
to depression (although this may not manifest itself until
many years later). What happens is that such infants achieve
their sense of unity and harmony with the depressed mother
not by means of their developmental achievements but by
producing the mother's mood in themselves.

All this means no more than that tendencies, inclinations,
predilections (including the tendency to depression, to masochistic attitudes, etc.) which are present in all human
beings can be eroticized and stimulated toward growth
through forming emotional links between the child and his
first object.

The disequilibrium between developmental lines which is
created in this manner is not pathological as such. Moderate
disharmony does no more than prepare the ground for the
innumerable differences as they exist among individuals
from an early date, i.e., it produces the many *variations of
normality* with which we have to count.

Applications:
Entry into Nursery School as an Illustration

To return to the problems and queries raised by parents which are mentioned above:

With the foregoing points in mind, the child analyst can cease to answer them on the basis of the child's chronological age, a factor which is inconclusive psychologically; or on the basis of the child's intellectual grasp of the situation, which is a one-sided view diagnostically. Instead, he can think in terms of basic psychological differences between the mature and immature, and in terms of lines of development. The child's readiness to meet events such as the birth of a sibling, hospitalization, school entry, etc., is seen then as the direct outcome of his developmental progress on all the lines which have a bearing on this specific experience. If the appropriate stations have been reached, the happening will be constructive and beneficial to the child; if this is not the case, either on all or on some of the lines concerned, the child will feel bewildered and overtaxed and no effort on the part of the parents, teachers, nurses will prevent his distress, unhappiness, and sense of failure which often assume traumatic proportions.

Such a "diagnosis of the normal child" can be illustrated by a practical example, taking—as one for many—the question under which developmental circumstances a child is ready to leave his home surroundings temporarily for the first time, to give up his close proximity to the mother and enter group life in a nursery school without undue distress and with benefit to himself.

REQUIRED STATUS ON THE LINE "FROM DEPENDENCY TO
EMOTIONAL SELF-RELIANCE"

In the not-too-distant past it was assumed that a child who
had reached the age of three years six months should be
able to separate from his mother on the first day of entry
at the outer door of the nursery school building and should
adapt to the new physical surroundings, the new teacher,
and the new playmates all in one morning. A blind eye was
turned toward the distress of the new entrants; their crying
for their mothers, their initial lack of participation and
cooperation were considered of little significance. What
happened under those conditions was that most children
went through an initial stage of extreme unhappiness, after
which they settled down to nursery school routine. Some
others reversed this sequence of events. They began with a
period of acquiescence and apparent enjoyment which
then, to the surprise of parents and teacher, was followed
a week later by intense unhappiness and a breakdown in
participation. In their case, the delayed reaction was due
to a slower intellectual grasp of the external circumstances.
What seems important with regard to both types of reaction is the fact that formerly no thought was given to the
way the individual children were affected internally by their
respective periods of distress and desolation, and—more
important still—that the latter were accepted as inevitable.

As seen from our present point of view, they are inevitable only if developmental considerations are neglected.
If, at nursery school entry, a child of whatever chronological age still finds himself at stage one or two of this developmental line, separation from home and mother, even
for short periods, is not age adequate and offends against

his most vital need; protest and suffering under these conditions are legitimate. If he has reached *object constancy* at least (stage 3), separation from the mother is less upsetting, he is ready to reach out to new people and to accept new ventures and adventures. Even then, the change has to be introduced gradually, in small doses, the periods of independence must not be too long, and, in the beginning, return to the mother should be open to his choice.

REQUIRED STATUS ON THE LINE TOWARD BODILY INDEPENDENCE

Some children are extremely uncomfortable in nursery school because they find themselves unable to enjoy any food or drink which they are given, or to use the lavatory for urination or defecation. This does not depend on the type of food offered or on the lavatory arrangements themselves, although the child himself usually uses their strangeness as a rationalization. The real difference between the child's function or disfunction in these respects is the developmental one. On the eating line at least stage 4 of self-feeding should have been reached; on the line to bowel and bladder control, the attitude toward cleanliness belonging to stage 3.

REQUIRED STATUS ON THE LINE TOWARD COMPANIONSHIP

Any child will be a disturbing element in the nursery school group, and unhappy in himself, before he has attained the stage where other children can be related to at least as helpmates in play (stage 3). He will be a constructive, leading member in the group as soon as he learns to accept other children as partners in their own right, a step which enables him also to form real friendships (stage 4). In fact, if development in this respect is at a lower level, he either should not be accepted in nursery school or, if he has entered, he should be permitted to interrupt attendance.

REQUIRED STATUS ON THE LINE FROM PLAY TO WORK

The child usually enters nursery school at the beginning of the stage when "play material serves ego activities and the fantasies underlying them" (stage 4), and he climbs up the ladder of development gradually through the sequence of toys and materials until at the end of nursery school life he reaches the beginning of "work," which is a necessary prerequisite for entry into elementary school. In this respect it is the task of the teacher throughout to match the child's needs for occupation and expression with the material offered and not to create a sense either of boredom or of failure by lagging too far behind or by anticipating needs before they arise.

So far as the child's ability to *behave* adequately in nursery school is concerned, this depends not on any of the developmental lines described, but in general on the interrelations between his id and ego. .

Somewhere in her mind, even the most tolerant nursery school teacher carries the image of the "ideal" nursery child who exhibits no outward signs of impatience or restlessness; who asks for what he wants instead of grabbing it; who can wait for his turn; who is satisfied with his fair share; who does not throw temper tantrums but can stand disappointments. Even if no single child will ever display all these forms of behavior, they will be found in the group, in one or the other pupil, with regard to one or the other aspect of daily life. In analytic terms this means that, at this period, the children are on the point of learning how to master their affects and impulses instead of being at the mercy of them. The developmental tools at their disposal in this respect belong above all to ego growth: advance from primary process to secondary process functioning, i.e., to be able to interpolate thought, reasoning, and anticipation of the future between wish and action directed toward fulfillment (Hartmann, 1947); advance from the pleasure principle to the reality principle. What comes to the help of the child from the side of the id is the age-adequate— probably organically determined—lessening in the urgency of the drives.

What will be discussed presently, in connection with the child's normal "regression rate" (Ernst Kris, 1950, 1951), is the fact that no young child should be expected to maintain his best level of performance or behavior for any length of time. But such temporary declines in the level of functioning, even if they occur easily and frequently, do not affect a child's eligibility for nursery school entrance.

III

REGRESSION AS A PRINCIPLE IN NORMAL DEVELOPMENT

Developmental lines and their disharmonies, as described above, are not themselves responsible for all the complexities which arise in childhood, especially not for all the obstacles and arrests which hinder its smooth course.

That there is progressive growth from the state of immaturity to maturity, along lines which are prescribed innately but influenced and shaped at every step by environmental conditions is a notion with which we are familiar from the processes of growth on the organic side where the anatomical, physiological, and neurological processes are in constant flux. What we are used to see in the body is that growth proceeds in a straightforward, progressive line until adulthood is reached, invalidated only by severe intervening illness or injury and, finally, by the destructive, involutionary processes of old age.

There is no doubt that a similar progressive move underlies psychic development, i.e., that in the unfolding of drive action, impulses, affects, reason, and morality, the individual also sets out on specifically prescribed paths and, subject to environmental circumstances, pursues them to their conclusion. But the analogy between the two fields does not carry further than this point. While on the physical side, normally, progressive development is the only innate force in operation, on the mental side we invariably have to count with a second, additional set of influences which work in the opposite direction, namely, with fixations and regressions. It is only the recognition of both movements, progressive and regressive ones, and of the interactions between them, that leads to satisfactory explanations of the happenings on the developmental lines described above.

Three Types of Regression

In an addition (1914) to the *Interpretation of Dreams* (1900) the distinction was made between three types of regression: (a) a *topographical* regression in which excitation moves in a backward direction from the motor end to the sensory end of the mental apparatus until it reaches the perceptual system; this is the regressive process which produces hallucinatory wish fulfillment in the place of rational thinking; (b) a *temporal* regression as a harking back to older psychic structures; (c) a *formal* regression which causes primitive methods of expression and representation to take the place of the contemporary ones. It is stated in the same connection that those "three kinds of regression are . . . one at bottom and occur together as a rule; for what is older in time is more primitive in form and in psychical topography lies nearest to the perceptual end" (p. 548). In spite of their similarities, for our present purposes the actions of the various kinds of regression seem sufficiently distinct to be discussed and treated separately with regard to different parts of the immature individual's personality and even to be subdivided further.

To facilitate thinking in our current metapsychological language, I begin by translating the earlier topographical concept of the mental apparatus into the later structural terms. The quotation from the *Interpretation of Dreams* then reads as follows: that regression can occur in all three parts of the personality structure, in the id as well as in the ego and superego; and that it can concern psychic content as well as methods of functioning; that *temporal* regression happens in regard to aim-directed impulses, object representations, and fantasy content; *topographical* and *formal* regression in the ego functions, the secondary thought processes, the reality principle, etc.

Regression in Drive and Libido Development

Most closely studied in analysis is temporal regression in drive and libido development. What is affected here, on the one hand, is the choice of objects and the relations to them, with consequent returns to those of earliest significance and the most infantile expressions of dependence. On the other hand, the drive organization may be affected as a whole and reverting to earlier pregenital levels and to the aggressive manifestations coordinated with them may be brought about. Regression in this respect is considered as based on a specific characteristic of drive development, namely, on the fact that while libido and aggression move forward from one level to the next and cathect the objects which serve satisfaction on each stage, no station on the way is ever fully outgrown, as it is on the organic side. While one part of the drive energy is on a forward course, other portions of it, of varying quantity, remain behind, tied to earlier aims and objects, and create the so-called *fixation points* (to autoerotism and narcissism, to the stages of the infant-mother relationship, preoedipal and oedipal dependency, to oral pleasures and oral sadism, to anal-sadistic or passive-masochistic attitudes, phallic masturbation, exhibitionism, egocentricity, etc.). Fixation points may be caused by any type of traumatic experience, by either excessive frustration or excessive gratification on any of these levels, and may exist with different degrees of awareness and consciousness or repression and unconsciousness attached to them. For the developmental outcome this is less important than the fact that for whatever cause and in either state they have the function of binding and retaining drive energies and that thereby they impoverish later drive functioning and object relations.

Fixations and regressions have always been regarded as interdependent.[8] By virtue of their very existence and according to the measure of libido and aggression with which they are cathected, the fixation points exert a constant retrograde pull on drive activity, an attraction which makes itself felt during all early development and in maturity.

The intricacies of *sexual* regression can be shown best in any clinical instance which is dissected and described in detail, although the statements concerning them are usually unduly abbreviated and therefore incomplete. Thus, it is not enough to say that a boy on the phallic-oedipal level under the impact of castration anxiety "has regressed to the anal or oral phase." What has to be described additionally is the form, scope, and significance of the regressive movement which has taken place. The statement may mean in its simplest form no more than that the boy has retreated from rivalry with the father and from the fantasy of possessing the oedipal mother and has reactivated his pre-oedipal conception of her with the corresponding clinging,

[8] "The stronger the fixations on its [the libido's] path of development, the more readily will the [later] function evade external difficulties by regressing to the fixations" (S. Freud, 1916-1917, p. 341).

demanding, torturing attitudes, while otherwise everything remains the same: that he continues to regard her as a whole person in her own right and continues to discharge the anal and oral excitations connected with her in the act of phallic masturbation. Or the same statement may imply that regression has also affected the level of object relatedness itself. In that case object constancy is given up and what is revived are the anaclitic (or part object) attitudes: the personal importance of the love object becomes overshadowed again by the importance of satisfying a component instinct, a relationship which is normal for the toddler period but which—at later ages and in maturity— produces shallowness and promiscuity in object relations. There is a third possibility that regression may also include the method of discharging sexual excitement; where this happens, phallic masturbation disappears altogether and is replaced by impulses to eat, to drink, to urinate or to defecate at the height of excitation.

The most serious manifestations are those, obviously, where all three forms of sexual regression (of object, aim, and method of discharge) occur simultaneously.[9]

---

[9] During the actual process of child analysis it is easy to distinguish between the boy patients who produce (or fight to suppress) an erection at significant moments and those others who instead have to escape to the lavatory to pass urine or feces or who urgently need a glass of water or to suck sweets.

That the method of discharging sexual excitation is of the highest significance for assessing the whole status of a child's sexual constellation was discussed by S. Freud in "An Infantile Neurosis" (1918, written in 1914): "The fact that our little boy passed a stool as a sign of his sexual excitement is to be regarded as a characteristic of his congenital sexual constitution. He at once assumed a passive attitude, and showed more inclination towards a subsequent identification with women than with men" (p. 81).

Regressions in Ego Development

In our work as analysts we have become so familiar with this constant interplay between drive fixations and regressions that we have to guard against the almost automatic mistake to view the regressive processes on the side of ego and superego in corresponding terms. While the former are determined above all by the stubborn adhesion of the drives to all objects and positions which have ever yielded satisfaction, characteristics of this kind play no part in ego regression, which is based on different principles and follows different rules.

TEMPORARY EGO REGRESSIONS IN NORMAL DEVELOPMENT

The backward moves which occur in every child's normal development of functioning are well known to all those who deal with young children and their upbringing in practical capacities. By the latter, regression of function is taken for granted as a common characteristic of infantile behavior.[10]

Actually, when studied in detail, regressive tendencies can be shown to occur with regard to all the important achievements of the child: in the ego functions of control of motility, reality testing, integration, speech; in the acquisition of bowel and bladder control; in the secondary thought processes and mastery of anxiety; in the elements of social adaptation such as frustration tolerance, impulse control, manners; in superego demands such as honesty, fairness in dealing with others, etc. In all these respects, an

[10] There is a popular saying that "children take two steps forward and one backward."

individual child's capacity to function on a comparatively high level is no guarantee that the performance will be stable and continuous. On the contrary: occasional returns to more infantile behavior have to be taken as a normal sign. Thus, nonsense talk or even babbling have a rightful place in the child's life, alongside rational speech and alternating with it. Clean toilet habits are not acquired at one go, but take the long back-and-forth way through an interminable series of successes, relapses, accidents. Constructive play with toys alternates with messing, destructiveness, and erotic body play. Social adaptation is interrupted periodically by reversals to pure egoism, etc. In fact, what we regard as surprising are not the relapses but occasional sudden achievements and advances. Such moves forward may occur with regard to feeding where they take the form of a sudden refusal of the breast and transition to bottle, spoon or cup, or from liquids to solids; or at later ages a sudden relinquishing of food fads. They are known to happen with regard to habits as a sudden giving up of thumb sucking or of a transitional object, of fixed sleeping arrangements, etc. In toilet training, instances are known of almost instantaneous change-over from wetting and soiling to bladder and bowel control; with regard to aggression, its almost overnight disappearance with change-over to shy, restrained, diffident behavior. But convenient as such transformations may be for the child's environment, the diagnostician views them with suspicion and ascribes them not to the ordinary flow of progressive development but to traumatic influences and anxieties which unduly hasten its normal course. According to experience, the slow method of trial and error, progression and temporary reversal is more appropriate to healthy psychic growth.

DETERIORATION OF SECONDARY PROCESS FUNCTIONING IN THE
WAKING LIFE OF CHILDREN

This practical acknowledgment of the ubiquity of ego regressions in the child's normal life was not matched for
many years by a corresponding treatment of the subject
in the analytic literature. Personally, I myself was interested
in it long ago and brought it to the attention of the Vienna
Society in the '30s in a short paper entitled "Deterioration
of Secondary Process Functioning in the Waking Life of
Children." I summarized there that such deteriorations
manifest themselves in a number of situations which have
in common the factor that ego control of mental functioning is lessened for one reason or another, as in the following:

(a) In *child analysis*, as in every analytic setting, arrangements are made with the intention to prompt the child to
reduce his defenses and controls and increase the freedom
of fantasies, impulses, preconscious and unconscious processes. Under these conditions it can be shown how the
child's play and his verbal expressions gradually lose the
characteristics of secondary process thinking such as logic,
coherence, rationality, and display instead characteristics of
primary process functioning such as generalizations, displacements, repetitiveness, distortions, exaggerations. A certain central theme which, initially, is found in its logical
place in a fantasy or game may run wild and attach itself
to every element of the construction, however forced and
unfitting the connection; or it may be intensified until it
becomes absurd. To take examples from past and present
analytic work: a five-year-old, in his play with "little world"
toys, staged the element of "fighting" quite tentatively and

soberly by letting the small family dolls engage in quarrels with each other; but as the play progressed, the element of fighting slipped out of control and passed from the people to the inanimate objects until at the climax all the furniture was involved and the kitchen sink engaged in a wild "hand to hand" battle with the table and cupboards. Similarly, a boy's drawing of a battleship may contain perhaps one or two guns placed in the correct position, while the productions which follow increase the number and place them anywhere until the whole ship, over and under water, bristles with them.[11] Items such as biting, which appear first in a fantasy attached to some wild animal such as tiger or crocodile, may leave the place where they are "bound" by symbolic representation and, once set free of ego control, manifest themselves everywhere, with everybody and everything biting each other, etc.

(b) Almost identical manifestations can be shown to occur outside the analytic setting in the normal child's behavior at *bedtime* in the transition period from active waking life to falling asleep, when even the most reasonable and well-adapted children begin to fret, to whine, to talk nonsense, to cling, and to demand the physical attentions which they used to receive at much younger ages. Here too, what impresses one especially is the growing disorder in the thought processes, the perseveration of single words or sentences, the general lability of affects shown in the almost instantaneous mood swings from hilarity to crying. For the student of regression, there can scarcely be a more convincing picture of the ego deteriorating gradually and failing to perform one function after the other until

[11] This, of course, has also a defensive character which is neglected here.

finally all ego functioning is suspended and sleep intervenes.

(c) Actually, my first encounter with such manifestations happened much earlier, when I was still *in school*. I remember vividly being myself a member of a class of sixth formers who were overstrained due to a timetable which arranged for a series of difficult subjects in succession without sufficient intervening breaks. Eminently sensible and attentive as we were at the beginning of the morning, this invariably broke down in the fifth or sixth hour when even the most innocent words uttered by anybody produced wild outbursts of giggles and uncontrolled behavior. The male teachers who had the misfortune to take the class at this time would indignantly denounce the whole roomful of girls as "a flock of silly geese." I realized that we were tired and it puzzled me that this should make us silly, but all I could do then was to file the fact in my memory to come up for later explanation.

OTHER EGO REGRESSIONS UNDER STRESS

Even though my descriptions aroused little or no interest in the Vienna Society at the time (and remained unpublished), the whole subject was taken up again at a later date by a number of analytic authors. After watching the behavior of young children in nursery school, Ernst Kris introduced the concept and term "regression rate." He demonstrated with examples that the younger the child, the shorter is the period during which his performance keeps at the optimal level. This explains a fact, empirically well known to nursery school teachers, why their pupils will function less well at the end of the morning than in the beginning and why these regressions concern the handling of play material (return from the stage of ego-dominated constructive play to the stage of impulse-dominated messy, aggressive, and destructive play); the social relations (return from partnership and considerateness to egoism and quarrelsomeness); and the tolerance for frustration (lessening of ego control over impulses with resultant increase in the urgency of drive activity).

A number of other publications emphasized other stress situations besides tiredness as the operative factors in the regression of functioning, although in these cases ego regression usually appears coupled with simultaneous drive regression, or as a preliminary or a consequence of the latter. Such papers referred, on the one hand, to the influence of *bodily pain*, fever, physical discomfort of any kind and made the point that concerning feeding and sleeping habits, toilet training, play and general adaptedness, children in illness have to be regarded and treated as potentially regressed children, with much of their age-adequate functioning reduced or in abeyance (Anna Freud, 1952). On the other hand, much attention began to be paid from the 1940s onward to the corresponding effect of psychic pain in traumatic situations, anxiety, and above all in the distress caused by a young child's separation from his first love objects (separation anxiety). The severe libidinal and ego regressions caused by this have been described at length for wartime nurseries, other residential institutions, hospitals, etc.[12]

There is one distinguishing characteristic of ego regression to be noted, irrespective of the various causative fac-

[12] See in this respect A. Freud and D. Burlingham (1943, 1944), John Bowlby (1960), James Robertson (1958), René Spitz (1945, 1946), and others.

tors. In contrast to drive regression, the retrograde moves on the ego scale do not lead back to previously established positions, since no fixation points exist. Instead, they retrace the way, step by step, along the line which had been pursued during the forward course. This is borne out by the clinical finding that in ego regression it is invariably the most recent achievement which is lost first.[13]

EGO REGRESSIONS AS THE RESULT OF DEFENSE ACTIVITY

Another type of lowering of ego function deserves to be described as "regression," although it is usually not included in this category.

As the ego of the child grows and improves its functioning, better *awareness* of the internal and external world brings it into contact with many unpleasurable and painful aspects; the increasing dominance of the *reality principle* curtails wishful thinking; the improvement of *memory* leads to retaining not only pleasurable but frightening and painful items; the *synthetic function* prepares the ground for conflict between the inner agencies, etc. The resultant influx of unpleasure and anxiety is more than the human being can bear without relief; consequently it is warded off by the defense mechanisms which come into action to protect the ego.

Thus, *denial* interferes with accuracy in the perception of the outer world by excluding the unpleasurable. *Repression* does the same for the inner world by withdrawing conscious cathexis from unpleasurable items. *Reaction formations* replace the unpleasurable and unwelcome by the

---

[13] See the observations made on loss of speech, of toilet training, etc., in infants separated from their mothers.

opposite. All three mechanisms interfere with memory, i.e., with its impartial functioning, regardless of pleasure and unpleasure. *Projection* runs counter to the synthetic function by eliminating anxiety-arousing elements from the image of the personality and attributing them to the object world.

In short, while the forces of maturation and adaptation strive toward the increasing, reality-governed efficiency in all ego functioning, the defense against unpleasure works in the opposite direction and, in its turn, invalidates the ego functions. In this area too, therefore, constant forward and backward movements, progression and regression, alternate and interact with each other.

Drive and Ego Regressions, Temporary and Permanent

It is implied in the foregoing that regressions of the drives as well as of the ego and superego are normal processes which have their origin in the immature individual's flexibility. They are useful answers to the strain of a given moment and are always available to the child as responses to situations which otherwise might prove unbearable.[14] Thus, they serve simultaneously adaptation and defense, and in both functions help to maintain the state of normality.

What has not been emphasized sufficiently, so far, is that this beneficent aspect of regression refers only to those instances where the process is temporary and spontaneously reversible. Impairment of function due to tiredness then disappears automatically after rest or sleep; if due to frustration, pain, distress, the age-adequate drive positions or methods of ego functioning reinstate themselves as soon

[14] According to a formulation by René Spitz.

as the cause of strain has been removed, or, at least, soon afterwards.[15] But it would be unduly optimistic on our part to expect such a favorable turn of events in the large majority of cases. It happens just as often, especially after traumatic distresses, anxieties, illnesses, etc., that regressions, once embarked on, become permanent; the drive energies then remain deflected from their age-adequate aims, and ego or superego functions remain impaired, so that any further progressive development is severely damaged. Where this happens, regression ceases to be a beneficent factor in normal development and becomes a pathogenic agent. Unluckily, in our clinical appraisal of regressions as ongoing processes, it is almost impossible to determine whether in a given child's case the dangerous step from temporary to permanent regression has already been taken or whether spontaneous reinstatement of formerly reached levels is still to be expected. Thus far, I know of no criteria for this, even though the entire decision about the child's abnormality may depend on this distinction.

Regression and the Developmental Lines

To return once more to the concept of developmental lines:

Once we accept regression as a normal process, we also accept that movement along these lines is in the nature of a two-way traffic. During the whole period of growth, then, it has to be considered legitimate for children to revert periodically, to lose controls again after they have been established, to reinstate early sleeping and feeding patterns

[15] After illness, hospitalization, separation, there are time lags of varying lengths between the return of normal external conditions and the regaining of age-adequate drive and ego levels.

(for example, in illness), to seek shelter and safety (especially in anxiety and distress) by returning to early forms of being protected and comforted in the symbiotic and pre-oedipal mother relationship (especially at bedtime). Far from interfering with forward development, it will be beneficial for its freedom if the way back is not blocked altogether by environmental disapproval and by internal repressions and restrictions.

To the disequilibrium in the child's personality which is caused by development on the various lines progressing toward maturity at different speeds, we have to add now the unevennesses which are due to regressions of the different elements of the structure and of their combinations. On this basis it becomes easier to understand why there is so much deviation from straightforward growth and from the average picture of a hypothetically "normal" child. With the interactions between progression and regression being as complex as they are, the disharmonies, imbalances, intricacies of development, in short, the *variations of normality*, become innumerable.

CHAPTER 4

Assessment of Pathology
Part I. Some General
Considerations

Within the framework of our analytic thinking we regard the transition from the variations of normality to the emergence of pathology proper to be a quantitative step as often as a qualitative one. We see the mental equilibrium of human beings as based on the one hand on certain fixed relations between the inner agencies within their structure, and on the other hand between their entire personalities and the conditions of the environment. These relations are altered by any increase or decrease in the id derivatives, as they occur spontaneously in the latency period, in adolescence, in the climacterium; by any weakening of the ego and superego forces, as they happen under strain, in extreme tiredness, in many illnesses, regularly in old age; and by the changes in the opportunities for obtaining satisfac-

tion, as they are occasioned by object loss and other externally imposed deprivations and frustrations. The ease with
which the balance is upset has led to the view "That no
sharp line can be drawn between 'neurotic' and 'normal'
people, . . . that our conception of 'disease' is a purely practical one and a question of summation, that predisposition
and the eventualities of life must combine before the thresh-
old of this summation is overstepped, and that consequently a number of individuals are constantly passing from
the class of healthy people into that of neurotic patients,
while a far smaller number also make the journey into the
opposite direction" (S. Freud, 1909, p. 145f.).

While this statement is meant to cover people of all
ages "whether children or adults" (ibid.), it is obvious that
the demarcation line between mental health and illness is
even more difficult to draw in childhood than in later stages.
In the picture of the child's growth toward maturity, as
given in the previous chapter, it is inherent that the proportion of strength between id and ego is in constant flux;
that adaptive and defensive, beneficial and pathogenic processes merge into each other; that the transitions from one
developmental level to the next constitute points of potential arrest, malfunction, fixation and regression; that id
derivatives and ego functions, and with them the main
developmental lines, grow at uneven rates; that temporary
regressions may become permanent; in short, that there are
a number of factors which combine to undermine, arrest,
distort, and deflect the forces on which mental growth is
based.

In this constantly shifting internal scene of the developing individual, the current diagnostic categories are of little

help and increase rather than decrease the confusing aspects of the clinical picture.

In recent years, child analysis has advanced decisively in a variety of directions. So far as technical procedure is concerned, it has achieved more or less independent status, in spite of many initial setbacks and difficulties. In the area of theory, findings have been made which are recognized as true additions to, not merely confirmations of, the body of psychoanalytic knowledge. But to date, this adventurous and even revolutionary spirit of the child analyst has exhausted itself in the areas of technique and theory, and has stopped short of the important question of classification of disorders. Here, a wholly conservative policy has been pursued, i.e., diagnostic categories have been taken over wholesale not only from the field of adult analysis but, beyond this, from adult psychiatry and criminology. The whole psychopathology of childhood has been fitted, more or less forcibly, into these existing patterns.

There are many reasons why, in the long run, this solution of the diagnostic question proves unsatisfactory as a basis for assessment, prognosis, and selection of therapeutic measures.

DESCRIPTIVE VERSUS METAPSYCHOLOGICAL ASSESSMENTS

As in the field of adult analysis, the descriptive nature of many of the current diagnostic categories runs counter to the essence of psychoanalytic thinking, since it emphasizes the identity of or difference between manifest symptomatology while neglecting those of the underlying pathogenic factors. It is true that in this manner a classification of disturbances is achieved which seems orderly and comprehensive to the superficial glance. But such a schema does nothing to advance deeper understanding or to promote differential diagnoses in a metapsychological sense. On the contrary, whenever the analyst accepts diagnostic thinking on this level, he is inevitably led into confusion in assessment and subsequently to erroneous therapeutic inferences.

To name a few examples in place of many: terms such as temper tantrum, truancy, wandering, separation anxiety, etc., subsume under the same heading a variety of clinical pictures in which behavior and symptomatology are similar, although, according to their underlying metapsychological pathogenesis, they belong to totally different analytic categories and call for different therapeutic handling.

A *temper tantrum*, for instance, may be no more than the direct motor-affective outlet for chaotic drive derivatives in a young child; in this case, there is every chance that it will disappear as a symptom, without any form of treatment, as soon as speech and other more ego-syntonic channels of discharge have been established. Or, as a second possibility, the temper tantrum may be an aggressive-destructive outburst in which the hostile tendencies are, in part, deflected from the object world and lived out in a violent manner on the child's own body and his immediate inanimate surroundings (head knocking, kicking against furniture, walls, etc.); in this eventuality it is only the eliciting of the anger and its reconnection with the frustrating or otherwise offending person which will bring relief. Or, third, what appears as a temper tantrum may on closer inspection turn out to be an anxiety attack, as it occurs in the more highly organized personality structures of phobic children whenever their protective mechanisms are interfered with by the environment. Deprived of his defense, an agoraphobic child forced to go into the street or a child with an animal phobia faced with the object of his fear is exposed helplessly to massive and intolerable anxiety and he expresses this state in outbursts which descriptively may be indistinguishable from a simple temper tantrum. Nevertheless, unlike the temper tantrum, these anxiety attacks are relieved only either by the reinstatement of the defense or by the analytic tracing, interpretation, and dissolution of the original source of the displaced anxiety.

Similarly, a variety of disparate states is covered by the terms *truancy, vagrancy,* or *wandering.* Some children run away from home because they are maltreated, or because they are not tied to their families by the usual emotional bonds; or they run away from school or avoid school because they fear teacher or classmates, because their learning performance is bad, because they expect criticism, punishment, etc. Here, the cause of the deviant behavior is rooted in the external conditions of the child's life and is removed with improvement of the latter. In contrast to this simple situation, there are other children who wander or truant not for external but for internal reasons. They are under the domination of an unconscious urge which compels them to search for an imaginary goal, usually a lost object of the past, i.e., although descriptively they run *away* from their surroundings, in the deeper sense they are running *toward* the fulfillment of a fantasy. In their case, not management or improvement of the external circumstances but only the tracking down of the unconscious wish will remove the symptom.

Even the more recently coined term *separation anxiety* is descriptive rather than dynamic in its usage. In clinical diagnoses one hears it applied indiscriminately to the states of distress in separated infants as well as to the states of mind causing school phobias (i.e., the inability to leave home) or homesickness (a form of mourning) in latency children. Here also, to employ the same name for two sets of disorders with similar manifest appearances tends to obscure the essential metapsychological differences which are characteristic of them. To separate, for whatever reason, a young infant from his mother during the period of biological unity between them represents an unwarranted interference with major inherent needs. It is reacted to as such by the infant with legitimate distress which can be relieved only by the return of the mother or, in the longer run, by establishing a substitutive mother tie. There is no correspondence here, except in behavior, with the states of mind of the homesick or the school-phobic child. In these latter cases the distress experienced at separation from mother, parents, or home is due to an excessive ambivalence toward them. The conflict between love and hate of the parents can be tolerated by the child only in their reassuring presence. In their absence, the hostile side of the ambivalence assumes frightening proportions, and the ambivalently loved figures of the parents are clung to so as to save them from the child's own death wishes, aggressive fantasies, etc. In contrast to the separation distress of the infant, which is relieved by reunion with the parent, in ambivalence conflicts reunion with the parents acts merely as a palliative; here only analytic insight into the conflict of feelings will cure the symptom.

In short, thinking in descriptive terms, useful as it may be in its own area, becomes disastrous when taken as a starting point for analytic inferences.

STATIC VERSUS DEVELOPMENTAL TERMINOLOGY

Since diagnostic terms, as they are used at present, have been devised with the mental or social disturbances of adults in mind, they inevitably neglect questions of age and stage of development and do not sufficiently provide for the differences between symptoms which are caused by delay or failure to attain and perfect specific personality traits and symptoms which are caused by breakdown of function or transgressions against it. For the child analyst's assessment, on the other hand, such distinctions are vital. Forms of behavior such as lying and stealing, aggressive and destructive attitudes, perverse activities, etc., cannot be fitted adequately into any scheme of normality or pathology without the background of a fairly accurate timetable of developmental sequences.

Lying

At what age and stage of development, for instance, does the falsification of truth begin to deserve the name of *lying*, i.e., when does it assume the importance of a symptom with a distinct flavor of deviation from the social norm? Obviously, before this happens, a series of developmental prestages has to be passed during which truthfulness is not expected from the child. For the infant, it is normal to turn away from painful impressions in favor of pleasurable ones, to play down the former, and to ignore or *deny* them if they are persistent. There are similarities between this attitude, which is a primitive defense mechanism directed against the arousal of unpleasure, and the older child's or adult's distortion of objective facts. But it remains a matter of opinion in which way the two forms of behavior are related to each other and whether the former should be viewed with the expectation of the later developments in the diagnostician's mind. Wishful thinking and the domination of the pleasure principle—in short, the primary process in mental functioning—are the forces that in the young child militate against truthfulness in the adult sense of the word. The child analyst has to decide from when onward to use the term lying in his diagnostic statements and has to base his decision in this respect on clear-cut notions concerning the timing in ego development of steps such as the transition from primary to secondary process, the ability to distinguish between inner and outer world, reality testing, etc.

Some children take longer than others to perfect these ego functions and therefore continue to tell lies "in all innocence." Others complete this development normally, but are thrown back to earlier levels when they meet excessive frustrations and disappointments in the circumstances of their lives; they become so-called fantasy liars (pseudologia phantastica) who cope with intolerable realities by means of regression to infantile forms of wishful thinking. Finally, there are children who are well advanced in ego development but who have other than developmental reasons for avoiding or distorting the truth. Their motives are the gaining of material advantage, fear of authority, escape from criticism or punishment, wishes for aggrandizement, etc. In the child analyst's assessments, the term lying is reserved with advantage for these latter instances, the so-called delinquent lying.

In many of the actual cases seen in a children's clinic, the etiology consists of a combination of all three forms, i.e., innocent lying, fantasy lying, and delinquent lying, with the developmentally earlier forms acting as preconditions for the later ones. That such blending is common and frequent does not absolve the child analyst from the duty to disentangle the mixture and to determine to which degree each of the factors contributes to the final symptomatic result.

Stealing

There are very similar considerations which govern the use of the term *stealing*, a term which is legitimate in diagnostic assessment only after the concept of private property has become meaningful for the child. Here too, a sequence of developmental steps needs to be traced, which so far has been given little attention by analytic authors.

The attitude which makes the small infant grab everything he desires is usually attributed to his insatiable "oral greed," which, at this early age, is not limited by any ego barriers. More accurately described, it has two roots, one each on the id and ego side. On the one hand, it is simply the familiar functioning according to the pleasure principle which prompts the immature ego to assign to himself whatever is pleasurable while rejecting the unpleasurable as extraneous matter. On the other hand, it is the age-adequate lack of distinction between self and object which determines the response. It is well known that, at this early stage, an infant can handle or mouth parts of the mother's body as if they were his own, i.e., play with them autoerotically (the mother's fingers, hair, etc.); or he can lend her his own body parts to play with (his fingers in her mouth); or he may spoon-feed himself and her in alternation. Such actions are often misunderstood as proof of an early and spontaneous generosity of infants, instead of being taken for what they are, namely, the consequence of unformed ego boundaries. It is this same indiscriminate merging with the object world which turns every infant into a formidable, even though innocent, menace to other people's right of property.

The ideas of "mine" and "not mine," which are indispensable concepts for the establishment of adult "honesty," develop very gradually, keeping step with the infant's gradual progress toward achievement of individual status. They apply first, probably, to the child's own body, next to the parents, then to the transitional objects, all of which are cathected both narcissistically and with object love. Significantly enough, as soon as the concept of "mine" emerges in the child's mind, he begins to guard his possessions fiercely and jealously against any interference. The notion of "being deprived of" or "stolen from" is understood by him long before the opposite one, that other people's property has to be respected. Before the latter becomes meaningful, the child has to extend and intensify his relationships to his fellow beings and to learn empathy with their attachment to their property.

Whatever the rate of progress in this respect, the concepts of "mine" and "yours" as such have little influence over the young child's behavior, since they conflict with very powerful desires for appropriation. Oral greed, anal possessiveness, urges to collect and hoard, overwhelming need for phallic symbols, all turn young children into potential thieves, unless educational coercion, superego demands, and, with these, gradual shifts in id-ego balance work in the opposite direction, namely, toward the development of honesty.

Taking the foregoing considerations into account, the diagnostician has to clarify a number of points before assigning a given case of stealing to one category or the other. He has to ask whether the act is due to incompleted or arrested growth of individual status, of object relations, of empathy, or of superego formation (stealing by backward or deficient children); or, where initial development is intact, whether temporary regressions in any of these vital areas have taken place (stealing as a phase-bound, transitory symptom); or, whether the child has regressed permanently in one or the other relevant aspect, with stealing as the resulting compromise formation (neurotic symptom); or, finally, whether the reason lies exclusively in insufficient ego control over normal, unregressed wishes for possession, i.e., in defective social adaptation (delinquent symptom).

As with lying, many of the actual clinical incidents of stealing are of mixed etiology, i.e., they are caused by combinations of arrest, regression, and weakness of ego control. That all young delinquents begin their thefts with stealing from the mother's purse indicates the degree to which all stealing is rooted in the initial oneness of mine and thine, self and object.

CRITERIA FOR ASSESSING SEVERITY OF ILLNESS

The child analyst also finds himself in difficulties when he proceeds to measure the seriousness of a child's disturbance by means of the criteria which are commonly employed with adults, namely, a survey of existent symptoms, an assessment of the suffering caused by them, and the resultant interference with important functions. None of these are valid for children without far-reaching modification.

Above all, *symptom formation* in childhood does not necessarily carry the same significance which it does in adult life where typical "symptoms . . . give us our bearings when we make our diagnosis" (S. Freud, 1916-1917, p. 271). Many of the inhibitions, symptoms, and anxieties of children are produced not by processes which are truly pathological but, as will be shown later, by the strains and stresses which are inherent in development itself. Such inhibitions and symptoms commonly appear when a particular phase of growth makes unusually high demands on the child's personality and, if in the meantime they are not mishandled by the parents, they may disappear again as soon as adaptation to the developmental level has been achieved or when its peak has passed. It is true, of course, that the manifestation of a difficulty betrays the vulnerability of the child; that often the so-called spontaneous cure prepares the way merely for a new set of disorders which arise on the next level; also, that usually they do not disappear without leaving weaknesses in one or the other area which become significant for symptom formation in adult life. But it is not at all rare, even for fully established symptoms such as phobic avoidances, obsessional precautions, feeding and sleeping difficulties, to fade out between referral and investigation of a case, simply because the anxieties on which they are based have become insignificant in comparison with the threat represented by the clinical investigation. For the same reason, before and during treatment, rearrangements of manifest symptomatology are apt to occur at a moment's notice, which means that symptomatic improvement during therapy means even less with children than it does with adults.

Altogether, the symptomatology of immature individuals is much too unstable to be relied on in assessment.

The point in time when adults are judged to need treatment and decide to undergo it is usually determined by the intensity of the *suffering* which their disturbance causes them. In children, however, the factor of mental distress in itself is no certain indicator of the presence or absence of pathological processes or of their severity. We have long been familiar with the fact that children suffer less than adults from their symptoms, probably with the one exception of anxiety attacks, which they feel acutely. Many other pathological manifestations, notably the phobic and obsessional ones, successfully serve the avoidance of pain and unpleasure rather than causing it, while the resulting restrictions and interferences with ordinary life are resented by the family, not, as with adults, by the patient himself. Food fads, neurotic restrictions of food intake, sleeping disturbances, clinging, temper tantrums upset the mother but are considered as ego syntonic by the child so long as they can be expressed freely; where the parents interfere, their restraining action, not the symptom, is blamed by the child for causing the distress. Even bed wetting and encopresis are frequently ignored and their disturbing and humiliating nature denied by the afflicted child. Neurotic inhibitions are usually dealt with by a complete withdrawal of interest from the given area, i.e., by ego restriction and consequently by indifference toward the losses of enjoyment caused by them. The most seriously disturbed children, such as those with mental or moral deficiencies, retardations, autisms and childhood psychoses, are completely oblivious of their illness, with maximum distress, of course, caused to the parents.

There is another reason why the presence of suffering in itself is no reliable indicator of mental illness. Children suffer less than adults from their psychopathology, but suffer more than adults from the other stresses to which they are exposed. In sharp contrast to former conventional beliefs, it is now well known that mental distress is an inevitable by-product of the child's dependency and of the normal developmental processes themselves. Young children suffer acutely from whatever delays, rationing, and frustrations are imposed on their body needs and drive derivatives; they suffer owing to separations from their early love objects, for whatever reason they occur; owing to real or imagined disappointments at their hands. Intense distress is caused, naturally, by the jealousies and rivalries which are inseparable from the experiences within the oedipus complex; or by the anxieties inevitably aroused in connection with the castration complex, etc. Even the most normal child may feel deeply unhappy for one reason or another, for long or short periods, almost every day of his life. This is a legitimate reaction where the child's emotions and his sensitive appreciation of external impressions and events have developed adequately. In contrast to what we expect to meet in adults, it is the compliant and resigned children who arouse our suspicion that abnormal processes are at work in them. Clinical experience shows that infants who are too "good," i.e., who accept without protest even the most unfavorable external conditions, may do so because they are organically damaged in some way, defective in their ego development, or extremely passive on the side of their drives. Children who separate too easily from their parents may do so because they have failed to form normal relationships, whether the reasons for this are internal or external. Not to feel distress and anxiety when loss of love is threatened, is not a sign of health and strength in a child; on the contrary, it is often the first indication of autistic withdrawal from the object world. In later childhood, too, guilt and internal conflicts with the resultant distresses occur legitimately and are indispensable signs of normal progressive growth. Where they are absent, we suspect serious delays in the processes of identification, internalization, and introjection, i.e., in the structuralization of the personality. It is no compensation to find that such defects go together with a lessening of internal stresses.

Obviously, we have to become accustomed to the paradoxical situation that the correspondence between pathology and suffering, normality and equanimity, as it exists in adults, is reversed in children.

I merely repeat a point which I have previously (1945) emphasized when I warn analysts not to base any of their assessments of children on the degree of *impairment* of *functioning*, notwithstanding the fact that this is one of the most revealing criteria for the pathology of adults. There is in childhood no stable level of functioning in any area or at any time; that is, there are no fixed points from which to take our departure in assessment. As described above, in connection with the manifestations of regression, the child's level of performance fluctuates unceasingly. Owing to shifts in development and changes in degrees of internal and external pressure, optimal positions are repeatedly gained, lost, and reinstated. Such alternation between progression and regression is normal, and its consequences are temporary, even though the resultant losses in achievement and efficiency may occasionally strike the observer as ominous. On the whole, it is safe to insist that children of all ages should be permitted at times to function below the level of their potentialities without being automatically labeled as "backward," "regressed," or "inhibited."

The diagnostician of children may find it all the easier to comply with this demand since it is a moot point which areas of the child's activities should be singled out here as significant. Play, freedom of fantasy life, school performance, stability of object relations, social adaptation have, all of them, been suggested in turn as vital aspects. Nevertheless, not one of them can qualify as being on a par with the adult's two main vital functions: his capacity to lead a normal love and sex life and his capacity to work. As suggested before (1945), there is only one factor in childhood the impairment of which can be considered of sufficient importance in this respect, namely, the child's capacity to move forward in progressive steps until maturation, development in all areas of the personality, and adaptation to the social community have been completed. Mental upsets can be taken as a matter of course so long as these vital processes are left intact. They have to be taken seriously as soon as development itself is affected, whether slowed up, reversed, or brought to a standstill altogether.

ASSESSMENT BY DEVELOPMENT AND ITS IMPLICATIONS

It is obvious, in the light of the foregoing, that child analysts have to free themselves from those diagnostic categories which are rigid, static, descriptive, or for other reasons alien to their field. Only when they have done this, will they be able to look at the clinical pictures before them with new eyes and assess them according to their significance for the process of development. This implies redirecting their attention from the symptomatology of the patient to his position on the developmental scale with regard to drive, ego and superego development, to the structuralization of the personality (stable borders between id, ego, and superego), and to modes of functioning (progression from primary to secondary thought processes, from pleasure to reality principle), etc. It implies asking themselves whether the child under examination has reached developmental levels which are adequate for his age, whether and in what respects he has either gone beyond or remained behind them; whether maturation and development are ongoing as processes or to what degree they are affected as a result of the child's disturbance; whether regressions or arrests have intervened, and, if so, to which depth and on what level.

To find the answers to such questions, a scheme of average developmental norms for all aspects of the personality is needed, such as has been embarked on tentatively in the preceding chapter. The more complete the scheme becomes, the more successfully will the individual patient be measured against it with regard to evenness or unevenness of progression rate, harmony or disharmony between developmental lines, and temporariness or permanency of regressions.

Uneven Drive and Ego Progression

We expect pathological consequences to follow in cases where development proceeds at different speeds in different areas of the personality. One of these eventualities with which we are familiar forms part of the etiology of the obsessional neurosis, where ego and superego development are accelerated while drive development is slowed up, or at least is slow in comparison with it. The incompatibility between relatively high moral and aesthetic superego demands and relatively crude fantasies and drive derivatives leads to the internal conflict by which in turn the obsessional defense activity is set in motion.[1]

The opposite eventuality, namely, a slowing up of ego and superego development coupled with normal or forward progress of the drives, occurs at least as often, if not more frequently, in our present-day clinic population and is in part responsible for many of the atypical clinical pictures, borderline manifestations, etc. Where ego and superego are immature in comparison with the levels of drive activity, neither the appropriate emotional object relationships nor sufficiently strong social and moral concerns are available to bind and control the pregenital and aggressive drive components. In their sexual growth, such children reach the anal-sadistic level without sufficient ego maturation to convert and neutralize the pregenital trends, which belong to this phase, into valuable contributions to character formation, i.e., into the corresponding reaction formations and sublimations. Or they reach the phallic level without simultaneously developing the ego-determined object relationships which normally organize the otherwise disjointed phallic trends into the coherent picture of the oedipus complex. Or they reach physical maturity in adolescence before the

---

[1] See S. Freud (1913, p. 325): ". . . I suggest the possibility that a chronological outstripping of libido development by ego development should be included in the disposition to obsessional neurosis." Another reason for obsessional symptom formation, namely, one-sided drive regression, will be discussed later.

ego is ready for the emotional genital relationships which give psychic meaning to the sexual act, etc.

In short, while accelerated ego development leads to an increase in conflicts, to neurotic symptom formation, and to the obsessional character, accelerated drive development produces lack of control in matters of sex and aggression, insufficient integration of the personality, and impulsive personalities (Michaels, 1955).

Disharmony between Developmental Lines

As indicated above, we do not expect children to show a very regular pattern in their growth, and we are ready to make allowances if their achievements are more advanced in one area of their life than in another. Disharmony between developmental lines becomes a pathogenic agent only if the imbalance in the personality is excessive.

If this happens, children are sent to a diagnostic service, usually with a long string of complaints from home or school. They are "problems"; they are as disturbed in themselves as they are disturbing to others; they do not accept community standards and consequently do not fit into any type of community life.

Clinical investigation confirms that neither do they fit any of the commonly applied diagnostic labels. A possible way of coming nearer to understanding their abnormality is to use the stages on the various lines of development as an approximate scale of measurement.

If we do this, we find that their levels of achievement are altogether out of proportion with each other. The most instructive examples among them are children with exceptionally high verbal intelligence quotients which are coupled, not only in the familiar way with exceptionally low performance levels (raising the suspicion of organic damage), but with exceptional backwardness on the lines toward emotional maturity, toward companionship, toward body management. The resulting distortion of behavior is alarming, particularly in such areas as acting out of sexual and aggressive trends, profusion of organized fantasy life, clever rationalization of delinquent attitudes, and lack of control over anal and urethral tendencies. In the usual way, such cases are classified as "borderline" or "prepsychotic."

Another not infrequent combination is the child's inability to reach the final stages on the line from play to work, while emotional and social development, body management, etc., are intact and, so far as these are concerned, the child functions on an age-adequate level. Such children are referred to the clinics as failures in school, in spite of their good intelligence. In the usual diagnostic examination it is not easy to pinpoint the specific steps in id-ego interaction which they have failed to achieve, unless we look into them for the prerequisites of the right attitude to work such as control and modification of pregenital drive components; functioning according to the reality principle; and pleasure in ultimate results of activity. Sometimes all of these, sometimes one or the other are lacking. Descriptively, the children under discussion are usually classified as "lacking in concentration," as having a "short attention span," as "inhibited."

Permanent Regressions and Their Consequences

As discussed before (Chapter 3), regression ceases to be a beneficent factor in development if its results become permanent instead of being spontaneously reversible. In this case, the various agencies within the structure (id, ego, and superego) have to come to new terms with each other on the basis of the damage which has been done by the regression. It is these aftereffects of regression which have the most harmful repercussions on the personality and which have to be considered in their role as pathogenic agents.

Permanent regressions, not unlike temporary ones, can have their starting point in any area of the personality.

One of the possibilities is that the regressive moves *begin in ego and superego* and reduce both to a lower level of functioning and that, secondarily, the damage spreads from there to the id derivatives. Ego and superego, if regressed, have less controlling power and this becomes manifest in a weakening of "censorship," i.e., in the dividing line between id and ego and the general efficiency of the defenses of the ego. The results are impulsive behavior, break-through of affect and aggressive tendencies, frequent breaches of id control, and irruptions of irrational elements into the child's consciousness and formerly rational behavior. For the parents these are alarming developments which change a child's character almost beyond recognition for no apparent reason. In clinical investigation the deterioration which has taken place can usually be traced back to some excessive strain to which ego and superego have been subjected by happenings such as traumatic shock, anxiety-arousing internal or external events, separations, severe disappointments in the child's love objects, severe disillusionment with his objects of identification, etc. (Jacobson, 1946).

The other possibility is that regression *begins on the side of the id derivatives* and that its pathogenic influence spreads from there in the opposite direction. In this case, ego and superego are affected in one of two ways, depending on whether they *condone* the lowered drive activity or *object* to it.

In the clinical entities which belong to the *first instance*, ego and superego give in to the regressive pull exerted by the happenings on the side of the drives and react with regression of their own, that is, with a lowering of their standards and demands. In this way, internal conflict between id and ego is avoided and the drives remain *ego syntonic*. On the other hand, the child's total personality is affected and its whole level of maturity reduced, a circumstance which leads to many puzzling forms of infantile nontypical, delinquent, and borderline behavior. In clinical detail, the resulting disorders depend on the intensity of the regressive moves on both sides, on the particular drive components or ego and superego functions which are affected and, finally, on the new interactions between id and ego at the level at which regression comes to a halt.

Owing to the comparative weakness and immaturity of the infantile ego, such a spread of regression to both sides of the personality is more characteristic of childhood than it is of adults, although it is not wholly absent in the latter.

The *second instance* refers to those children whose ego and superego are better organized from an early age onward and who are able to stand firm in the face of regressed drive activity. In many respects their functions have reached what we call, with Hartmann (1950b), secondary ego autonomy, namely, a measure of independence from happenings in the id. Instead of condoning the crude sexual and aggressive fantasies and impulses which come into consciousness after the drive energy has regressed to the fixation points, these children are horrified by them, reject them with anxiety, and under the pressure of anxiety first use the various defense mechanisms and then, if defense fails, resort to compromise and symptom formation. In short, they develop the internal conflicts which lead to the familiar pictures of the various infantile neuroses. The anxiety hysterics, phobias, pavor nocturnus, the obsessions, rituals, bedtime ceremonials, inhibitions, character neuroses belong in this category.

The difference between ego-syntonic and ego-dystonic drive regression is illustrated best by reference to the regressions from the phallic to the anal-sadistic phase, as they occur typically in boys at the height of the castration fears aroused by the happenings within the oedipus complex.

The children in whom ego and superego regression follows closely on drive regression become, at this time, either dirtier or more aggressive, or more clinging-possessive, or more passive-feminine in their behavior, or exhibit a combination of these various attributes that are implied in the sexuality of the anal phase. For them it is characteristic that they do not mind falling back into attitudes which previously they had outgrown successfully.

Those other children whose ego agencies are strong enough to resist regression and who react with typical anxiety, guilt, and defense activity develop not the same neurotic symptoms or character traits in all cases, but a variety of them, according to the specific drive elements to which they object most strongly. Where the dirty, the sadistic, and the passive trends are rejected by ego and superego with equal intensity, the defense is spread over the whole field and the symptomatology is profuse. Where only one or the other is singled out, the symptoms will be restricted either to excessive cleanliness, pollution fears, washing compulsions, or to inhibition of activity and competition, to fears of being turned into a female, or to compensatory outbursts of aggressive masculinity, etc. In any case, the result is unmistakably *neurotic*, whether in the form of isolated obsessional symptoms or the beginnings of obsessional character formation.

It is true that in these cases, too, the ego is finally affected by regression and becomes more infantile; but this is a secondary happening due to the primitive defense mechanisms such as denial, magical thinking, isolation, undoing, which are brought into action in addition to the more age-adequate repressions and reaction formations. Also, this regression is limited to the ego functions. So far as level and severity of ego ideal and superego demands are concerned, there are no regressive moves; on the contrary, the ego continues to undergo the most painful contortions to fulfill these.

ASSESSMENT BY TYPE OF ANXIETY AND CONFLICT

In the course of normal growth, every child takes a series of steps which lead from the initial state of comparative undifferentiation to the final full structuralization of the personality into id, ego, and superego. Division between id and ego, with different modes of functioning and different aims and concerns valid for each, is followed by division within the ego, after which superego, ego ideal, and ideal self are given the role of guiding and criticizing the ego's thoughts and actions. Intactness or impairment of growth in this respect and the child's exact position on this vital line of development are revealed to the diagnostician by two kinds of overt manifestations: by the type of the child's conflicts, and by the prevalent type of his anxieties.

With regard to conflict there are three main possibilities. One is that child and environment are at cross-purposes with each other. This happens whenever, under the dictates of the pleasure principle, the child's ego sides with his id in the pursuance of need, drive, and wish fulfillment, while control of the id derivatives is left to the outside world. This is a legitimate state of affairs in early childhood before id and ego have decisively moved away from each other, but it is considered as "infantile" if it persists at a later age, or if the child regresses to it. The anxieties coordinated with this state and diagnostically characteristic of it are aroused by the external world and take different forms according to a chronological sequence which runs as follows: fear of annihilation due to loss of the caretaking object (i.e., separation anxiety during the period of biological unity with the mother); fear of loss of the object's love (after object constancy has been established); fear of criticism and punishment by the object (during the anal-sadistic phase when this fear is reinforced by projection of the child's own aggression); castration fear (in the phallic-oedipal period).

The second type of conflict comes into being after identification with the external powers and after introjection of their authority into the superego. The reasons for clashes may remain the same as before, namely, pursuance of drive and wish fulfillment, but the disagreements themselves now occur internally between ego and superego. On the side of the anxieties this is revealed manifestly through fear of the superego, i.e., guilt. For the diagnostician, the appearance of guilt feelings is the unmistakable sign that this all-important step in structuralization, namely, the setting up of a functioning superego, has taken place.

For the third type of conflict it is characteristic that external conditions have no bearing on it, either directly, as in the first type, or indirectly, as in the second type. Clashes of this kind are derived exclusively from the relations between id and ego and the intrinsic differences between their organizations. Drive representatives and affects of opposite quality, such as love and hate, active and passive, masculine and feminine trends, exist peacefully side by side in the id while the ego is immature. But they become incompatible with each other and turn into sources of conflict as soon as the synthetic function of the maturing ego is brought to bear on them. On the other hand, any quantitative increase in the urgency of drives is felt by the immature ego as a threat to its organization and becomes a source of conflict as such. These wholly internal conflicts arouse great amounts of anxiety in the child; but, unlike fear and guilt, this anxiety remains in the depth and is reliably identified only during analysis, not at the diagnostic stage.

A classification of conflicts as external, internalized, and truly internal helps toward grading in some order of severity those childhood disturbances which, essentially, are based on conflict. So far as therapy is concerned, it also explains why some cases are improved by management of environmental conditions (those based on external conflict); why others are accessible only to internal intervention but need no more than average periods of analysis (internalized conflicts); while a certain number of children need analytic treatment of very long duration and unusual intensity, and present the analyst with excessive difficulties (truly internal conflict) (see S. Freud, 1937).

ASSESSMENT BY GENERAL CHARACTERISTICS

The child analyst who has the task of assessing the significance of a child's disturbance in the present is invariably also expected to give some opinion regarding his chances of mental health or illness in the future. The basis for such predictions is found not only in the details of the existing infantile disorder but also in certain general characteristics of the personality which play an essential role in the upkeep of internal balance. These characteristics are part of the given individual's constitution, that is, they are either innate or acquired under the influence of the infant's first experiences. Since it is the ego that has to mediate within the self and between self and environment, these traits are for the most part ego characteristics. Such stabilizing factors are high tolerance for frustration; good sublimation potential; effective ways of dealing with anxiety; and a strong urge toward completion of development.

Frustration Tolerance and Sublimation Potential

Experience shows that a child's chances of remaining mentally healthy are closely connected with his reaction to the unpleasure which is released whenever drive derivatives remain unsatisfied. Children are very different in this respect, apparently from the outset. Some find any delay or rationing of satisfaction intolerable and protest against it with unhappiness, anger, and impatience; they insist on unchanged fulfillment of the original wish and reject all substitute satisfactions and compromises with necessity. Usually, this shows first in the feeding situation, but is carried over from there to later stages as a habitual response to any thwarting of desires. In contrast, other children stand the same amounts of frustration with comparative equanimity or systematically reduce whatever tension they experience by accepting substitute gratifications. This response is likewise carried from the earliest to the later stages.

Obviously, the former children are the endangered ones. The undiminished amounts of tension and anxiety with which their egos have to cope are kept in very precarious check by means of primitive defenses such as denial and projection, or are given outlet periodically in the form of chaotic outbursts of temper. There is a very short path from these devices to pathology, i.e., to the production of neurotic, delinquent, or perverse symptoms.

Children of the second type either remain undisturbed under the same conditions or find relief in healthy displacement and neutralization of drive energy, which they direct to aim-inhibited, available goals. There is no doubt that the capacity to sublimate acts as a valuable safeguard to their mental health.

Mastery of Anxiety

There is little difference between children with regard to the type of anxiety they experience since, as mentioned before, the various types of it are invariable by-products of the consecutive stages of biological union with the mother (separation anxiety); of object relatedness (fear of loss of love); of the oedipus complex (castration anxiety); of superego formation (guilt). It is not the presence or absence, the quality, or even the quantity of anxiety which allows predictions as to future mental health or illness; what is significant in this respect is only the ego's ability to deal with anxiety. Here, the differences between one individual and another are very great, and the chances of maintaining mental equilibrium vary accordingly.

Other circumstances being equal, children are more likely to fall victim to later neurotic disturbances if they are unable to tolerate even moderate amounts of anxiety. In this case, they have to deny and repress all external and internal dangers which are potential sources of anxiety; or to project internal dangers onto the external world, which makes the latter more frightening; or to retreat phobically from danger situations to avoid anxiety attacks. In short, they set up a pattern for later life in which freedom from manifest anxiety has to be achieved at any price, and this is done via the constant use of defensive attitudes which favor pathological results.

The children whose outlook for mental health is better are those who cope with the same danger situations actively by way of ego resources such as intellectual understanding, logical reasoning, changing of external circumstances, aggressive counterattack, i.e., by mastery instead of by retreat. Since they can deal with larger amounts of anxiety in this manner, they can correspondingly dispense with excessive defense activity, compromise formations, and symptomatology.[2]

---

[2] This active mastery of anxiety must not be confused with the well-known counterphobic tendencies of children. In the former, the ego deals directly and healthily with the danger itself, while in the latter the ego defends itself secondarily against established phobic attitudes.

Active mastery of anxiety was described most effectively by O. Isakower in his verbal report on a frightened child who said enviously: "Even soldiers have fears; but they are lucky, they do not mind being afraid."

Regressive versus Progressive Tendencies

While regressive as well as progressive forces exist in all children as legitimate elements of development, the proportion of strength between them varies from individual to individual. There are children for whom, from early on, every new experience holds out the promise of pleasure, whether it is a question of new tastes and consistencies in food; steps from dependence to independence in motility; moves away from the mother to new adventures, toys, playmates; the move from home to nursery school, school, etc. Their lives are dominated by the wishes to be "big," to "do what the grownups do," and the normal partial fulfillments of such wishes compensate them for the usual difficulties, frustrations, and disappointments which are encountered on the way. Children of the opposite kind experience growth on every level above all as deprivation of previous forms of gratification. They do not wean themselves when this step is age adequate, but cling to breast or bottle and turn being weaned into a traumatic event; they are fearful of the consequences of growing bigger, of venturing out, of meeting strangers, later of assuming responsibilities, etc.

The clinical distinction between the two types is made best by observing the children's reactions to some taxing life experience such as bodily illness, birth of a sibling, etc. Where the progressive tendencies outweigh the regressive ones, the child answers to prolonged periods of illness with maturing of his ego, or responds to the birth of a baby in the family by claiming the status and privileges of the "big" brother or sister. Where regression is stronger than progression, bodily illness makes the child more infantile and the birth of a sibling becomes a reason for the older child to give up his achievements and to desire for himself the status of the baby.

The preponderance of either progressive or regressive tendencies as a general characteristic of the personality influences the maintenance of mental health and, consequently, is of prognostic value. Children of the first type are helped to proceed with maturation, development, and adaptation by the pleasure gains which they experience on the way. Children of the latter type are more exposed to arrests on the transition points between developmental levels, more likely to establish fixation points, to have breakdowns of equilibrium, and to take recourse to symptom formation.

A METAPSYCHOLOGICAL PROFILE
OF THE CHILD

Fact finding during the process of assessment produces a mass of information made up of data of different value and referring to different areas and layers of the child's personality: organic and psychic, environmental, innate and historical elements; traumatic and beneficial events; past and present development, behavior, and achievements; successes and failures; defenses and symptomatology, etc. Although all the data that are elicited merit careful investigation, including later verification or correction in treatment, it is basic to analytic thinking that the value of no single item should be judged independently, i.e., not without the item being seen within its setting. Hereditary factors depend for their pathogenic impact on the accidental influences with which they interact. Organic defects such as bodily malformation, blindness, etc., give rise to the most varied psychological consequences according to the environmental circumstances and the mental equipment of the child. Anxiety, as described above, cannot be assessed sufficiently on the basis of either quality or quantity, since its pathogenic impact depends on the coping devices (Murphy, 1964) and defense resources of the ego. The child's tempers and irrational actions have to be checked against the behavior patterns offered by the family, and the evaluation of cases in which the child developed these forms of behavior independently must differ from those in which he adopted them via imitation and identification. Traumatic events should not be taken at their face value but should be translated into their specific meaning for the given child. Attributes such as heroism or cowardice, generosity or greed, rationality or irrationality have to be understood differently in different individuals, and judged in the light of their genetic roots, their phase and age adequateness, etc. Thus, any of the elicited elements, although identical in name, may be totally different in significance in a different personality setting. In the same way that these variables do not lend themselves to comparison with allegedly identical variables in other individuals, they also offer no reliable bases for diagnostic evaluation if seen out of context, i.e., unrelated to other areas of the personality structure.

In the analysts's mind, the whole bulk of material collected during the diagnostic procedure organizes itself into what may be called a comprehensive metapsychological profile of the child, i.e., a picture which contains dynamic, genetic, economic, structural, and adaptive data. This can be seen as the analyst's synthetic effort when dealing with disparate findings, or, conversely, as showing his diagnostic thinking broken up analytically into its component parts.

Profiles of this kind can be drawn up at various junctures, namely, after the first contact between child and clinic (preliminary diagnostic stage), during analysis (treatment stage), and after the end of analysis or follow-up (terminal stage). If this is done, the profile serves not only as a tool for the completion and verification of diagnosis but also as an instrument to measure treatment results, i.e., as a check on the efficacy of psychoanalytic treatment.

At the diagnostic stage, the profile for each case should be initiated by the referral symptoms of the child, his description, his family background and history, and an enumeration of the possibly significant environmental influences. From these it proceeds to the internal picture of the child which contains information about the *structure* of his personality; the *dynamic* interplay within the structure; some *economic* factors concerning drive activity and the relative strength of id and ego forces; his adaptation to reality; and some genetic assumptions (to be verified during and after treatment). Thus, broken up into items, an individual profile may look as follows:

Draft of Diagnostic Profile

I. REASON FOR REFERRAL (Arrests in Development, Behavior Problems, Anxieties, Inhibitions, Symptoms, etc.)

II. DESCRIPTION OF CHILD (Personal Appearance, Moods, Manner, etc.)

III. FAMILY BACKGROUND AND PERSONAL HISTORY

IV. POSSIBLY SIGNIFICANT ENVIRONMENTAL INFLUENCES

V. Assessments of Development

A. *Drive Development*

   1. Libido.—Examine and state

      (a) with regard to *phase development:*

         whether in the sequence of libidinal phases (oral, anal, phallic; latency; preadolescence, adolescence) the child has proceeded to his age-adequate stage, and especially beyond the anal to the phallic level;

         whether he has achieved phase dominance on it;

         whether, at the time of assessment, this highest level is being maintained or has been abandoned regressively for an earlier one;

      (b) with regard to *libido distribution:*

         whether the self is cathected as well as the object world, and whether there is sufficient narcissism (primary and secondary, invested in the body, the ego, or the superego) to ensure self-regard, self-esteem, a sense of well-being, without leading to overestimation of the self, undue independence of the objects, etc.; state degree of dependence of self-regard on object relations;

      (c) with regard to *object libido:*

         whether in the level and quality of object relationships (narcissistic, anaclitic, object constancy, preoedipal, oedipal, postoedipal, adolescent) the child has proceeded according to age;

         whether, at the time of assessment, the highest level reached is being maintained or has been abandoned regressively;

whether or not the existent object relationships correspond with the maintained or regressed level of phase development.

2. Aggression.—Examine the aggressive expressions at the disposal of the child:

(a) according to their quantity, i.e., presence or absence in the manifest picture;

(b) according to their quality, i.e., correspondence with the level of libido development;

(c) according to their direction toward either the object world or the self.

B. *Ego and Superego Development*

(a) Examine and state the intactness or defects of ego apparatus, serving perception, memory, motility, etc.

(b) Examine and state in detail the intactness or otherwise of ego *functions* (memory, reality testing, synthesis, control of motility, speech, secondary thought processes). Look out for primary deficiencies. Note unevennesses in the levels reached. Include results of intelligence tests.

(c) Examine in detail the status of the *defense organization* and consider:

whether defense is employed specifically against *individual drives* (to be identified here) or, more generally, against drive activity and instinctual pleasure as such;

whether defenses are *age adequate*, too primitive, or too precocious;

whether defense is *balanced*, i.e., whether the ego has at its disposal the use of many of the important mechanisms or is restricted to the excessive use of single ones;

whether defense is *effective*, especially in its dealing
with anxiety, whether it results in equilibrium or
disequilibrium, lability, mobility, or deadlock
within the structure;

whether and how far the child's defense against the
drives is dependent on the object world or independent of it (superego development).

(d) Note any secondary interference of defense activity
with ego achievements, i.e., the price paid by the
individual for the upkeep of the defense organization.[3]

VI. Genetic Assessments

(Regression and Fixation Points)

Since we assume that all infantile neuroses (and some
psychotic disturbances of children) are initiated by libido
regressions to fixation points at various early levels, the loca-
tion of these trouble spots in the history of the child is one
of the vital concerns of the diagnostician. At the time of
initial diagnosis such areas are betrayed:

(a) by certain forms of manifest *behavior* which are characteristic of the given child and allow conclusions as
to the underlying id processes which have undergone
repression and modification but have left an unmistakable imprint. The best example is the overt obses-

---

[3] The interaction of drive development with ego and superego
development can be assessed by using for this purpose the Developmental Lines (see Chapter 3) which give us an idea how the total
personality reacts to any one of the situations in life which pose
for the child an immediate problem of mastery. This can be done
either within the framework of the Profile (as Part V C) or as an
addendum to it.

sional character where cleanliness, orderliness, punctuality, hoarding, doubt, indecision, slowing up, etc., betray the special difficulty experienced by the child when coping with the impulses of the anal-sadistic phase, i.e., a fixation to that phase. Similarly, other character formations or attitudes betray fixation points at other levels, or in other areas. (Concern for health or safety of parents and siblings shows a special difficulty of coping with the death wishes of infancy; fear of medicines, food fads, etc., point to defense against oral fantasies; shyness to that against exhibitionism; homesickness to unsolved ambivalence, etc.);

(b) by the child's *fantasy activity*, sometimes betrayed accidentally in the diagnostic procedure, usually only available through personality tests. (During analysis, the child's conscious and unconscious fantasies provide, of course, the fullest information about the pathogenically important parts of his developmental history);

(c) by those items in the *symptomatology* where the relations between surface and depth are firmly established, not open to variation, and well known to the diagnostician, as are the symptoms of the obsessional neurosis with their known fixation points. In contrast, symptoms such as lying, stealing, bed wetting, etc., with their multiple causation, convey no genetic information at the diagnostic stage.

VII. Dynamic and Structural Assessments (Conflicts)

Behavior is governed by the interplay of internal with external forces, or of internal forces (conscious or unconscious) with each other, i.e., by the outcome of conflicts.

Examine the conflicts in the given case and classify them as:

(a) external conflicts between the id-ego agencies and the object world (arousing fear of the object world);

(b) internalized conflicts between ego-superego and id after the ego agencies have taken over and represent to the id the demands of the object world (arousing guilt);

(c) internal conflicts between insufficiently fused or incompatible drive representatives (such as unsolved ambivalence, activity versus passivity, masculinity versus femininity, etc.).

According to the predominance of any one of the three types it may be possible to arrive at assessments of:

(1) the level of maturity, i.e., the relative independence of the child's personality structure;

(2) the severity of his disturbance;

(3) the intensity of therapy needed for alleviation or removal of the disturbance.

VIII. ASSESSMENT OF SOME GENERAL CHARACTERISTICS

The whole personality of the child should be scrutinized also for certain general characteristics which are of possible significance in predicting the chances of spontaneous recovery and reaction to treatment. Examine in this connection the following areas:

(a) the child's frustration tolerance. Where (with respect to developmental age) the tolerance for tension and frustration is unusually low, more anxiety will be generated than can be coped with, and the pathological sequence of regression, defense activity, and symptom formation will be more easily set in motion. Where frustration tolerance is high, equilibrium will be maintained, or regained, more successfully;

(b) the child's sublimation potential. Individuals differ widely in the degree to which displaced, aim-inhibited, and neutralized gratification can recompense them for frustrated drive fulfillment. Acceptance of these former types of gratification (or freeing of the sublimation potential in treatment) may reduce the need for pathological solutions;

(c) the child's over-all attitude to anxiety. Examine how far the child's defense against fear of the external world and anxiety caused by the internal world is based exclusively on phobic measures and counter-cathexes which are themselves closely related to pathology; and how far there is a tendency actively to master external and internal danger situations, the latter being a sign of a basically healthy, well-balanced ego structure;

(d) progressive developmental forces versus regressive tendencies. Both are, normally, present in the immature personality. Where the former outweigh the latter, the chances for normality and spontaneous recoveries are increased; symptom formation is more transitory since strong forward moves to the next developmental level alter the inner balance of forces. Where the latter, i.e., regression, predominate, the resistances against treatment and the stubbornness of pathological solutions will be more formidable. The economic relations between the two tendencies can be deduced from watching the child's struggle between the active wish to grow up and his reluctance to renounce the passive pleasures of infancy.

IX. Diagnosis

Finally, it is the diagnostician's task to reassemble the items mentioned above and to combine them in a clinically meaningful assessment. He will have to decide between a number of categorizations such as the following:

(1) that, in spite of current manifest behavior disturbances, the personality growth of the child is essentially healthy and falls within the wide range of "variations of normality";

(2) that existent pathological formations (symptoms) are of a transitory nature and can be classed as byproducts of developmental strain;

(3) that there is permanent drive regression to previously established fixation points which leads to conflicts of a neurotic type and gives rise to infantile neuroses and character disorders;

(4) that there is drive regression as above plus simultaneous ego and superego regressions which lead to infantilisms, borderline, delinquent, or psychotic disturbances;

(5) that there are primary deficiencies of an organic nature or early deprivations which distort development and structuralization and produce retarded, defective, and nontypical personalities;

(6) that there are destructive processes at work (of organic, toxic, or psychic, known or unknown origin) which have effected, or are on the point of effecting, a disruption of mental growth.

CHAPTER 5

Assessment of Pathology Part II. Some Infantile Prestages of Adult Psychopathology

For the child analyst, the assessment of the child's state serves a variety of purposes. Some are practical concerns such as the decision for or against treatment and the choice of the most appropriate therapeutic method. Others are theoretical and represent attempts to learn more about the developmental processes themselves. Last but not least in importance are the efforts to formulate clearer pictures of the initial phases of those mental disorders which are known principally from their later stages,[1] and to clear the field by distinguishing between transitory and permanent pathological manifestations.

[1] According to a term introduced by Liselotte Frankl, to study "the natural history" of the adult disorders.

THE INFANTILE NEUROSES

There are various reasons why child analysts feel on safest ground when dealing diagnostically with this category. From the early analytic days onward, the infantile neurosis has been declared to be not only on a par with its adult counterpart but more than that: its prototype and model.

There are the assurances, in the basic analytic literature on the subject, that the neurosis of childhood has the significance "of being a type and a model" (S. Freud, 1909, p. 147) of adult neurosis; that the analyses of children's neuroses "afford us . . . as much help towards a proper understanding of the neuroses of adults as do children's dreams in respect to the dreams of adults" (S. Freud, 1918, p. 9); that their study "protects us from . . . misunderstanding . . . the neuroses of adults" (S. Freud, 1916-1917, p. 363); that "analysis regularly reveals it [a neurosis of later years] as a direct continuation of the [preceding] infantile illness" (*ibid.*, p. 364).

Further, a close correspondence has repeatedly been shown to exist between the manifest symptomatology of infantile and adult neuroses. In *hysteria*, what is common to both are free-floating anxiety and anxiety attacks; conversion into physical symptoms; vomiting and refusal of food; animal phobias, agoraphobia. Claustrophobia, however, is rare in children in whom, instead, situational phobias such as school phobia, phobia of the dentist, etc., play a prominent part. On the side of the *obsessional* neurosis, both children and adults show the painfully heightened ambivalence of feeling, the bedtime ceremonials, other rituals, washing compulsions, repetitive actions, questions, formulas; magic words and gestures, or magic avoidance of particular words and movements; compulsions to count and list, to touch or avoid touch, etc. With the *inhibitions*, inhibited play and learning in children correspond to similar restrictions of activity in later life; inhibition of exhibitionism, of curiosity, of aggression, of competition, etc., produces the same crippling effect on the individual's personality whether they occur early or late in life. In the neurotic *characters*, there is little difference between the budding hysterical, obsessional, or impulsive character in childhood and their later, full-grown equivalents.

More important even than these correspondences on the manifest level is the identity which can be shown to exist between the infantile and adult neuroses with regard to their dynamics. The classical etiological formula for both runs as follows: initial developmental progress to a comparatively high level of drive and ego development (i.e., for the child to the phallic-oedipal, for the adult to the genital level); an intolerable increase of anxiety or frustration on this position (for the child of castration anxiety within the oedipus complex); regression from the age-adequate drive position to pregenital fixation points; emergence of infantile pregenital sexual-aggressive impulses, wishes, and fantasies; anxiety and guilt with regard to these, mobilizing defensive reactions on the part of the ego under the influence of the superego; defense activity leading to compromise formations; resulting character disorders or neurotic symptoms which are determined in their details by the level of the fixation points to which regression has taken place, by the content of the rejected impulses and fantasies, and by the choice of the particular defense mechanisms which are being used.

In the early days of analytic practice, when only a small number of preselected children reached the analyst, it was expected that the majority of young patients would belong to the category of the infantile neuroses and—with Little Hans and the Wolf Man as their prototypes—could be summed up under the etiological formula given above. But this notion changed with the step from private practice to the opening of consultation centers and clinics for children, where a whole mass of unsorted case material arrived and claimed the analyst's attention.

There emerged first a disappointing discovery concerning a discrepancy between infantile and adult neurotics. While in adults the individual neurotic symptom usually forms part of a genetically related personality structure, this is not so with children. In children, symptoms occur just as often in isolation, or are coupled with other symptoms and personality traits of a different nature and unrelated origin. Even well-defined obsessional symptoms such as bedtime ceremonials or counting compulsions are found in children with otherwise uncontrolled, restless, impulsive, i.e., hysterical, personalities; or hysterical conversions, phobic trends, psychosomatic symptoms are found in character settings which are obsessional. Single delinquent acts are committed by children who are well adapted and otherwise conscientious. Children who are out of control at home submit to authority in school, and vice versa.

Another disappointment was the realization that in spite of all the links between infantile and adult neuroses, there is no certainty that a particular type of infantile neurosis will prove to be the forerunner of the same type of adult neurosis. On the contrary, there is much clinical evidence which points in the opposite direction. An example is the uncontrolled state of a four-year-old which equals in many ways that of a juvenile or adult delinquent in so far as both give free rein to their impulses, especially the aggressive ones, and both attack, destroy, and appropriate what they desire without regard for other people's feelings. For all this similarity, this early delinquent behavior need not turn later into a true delinquent state; the child in question may develop into an obsessional character or obsessional neurosis rather than into a delinquent or criminal. Many children who begin with a phobia or anxiety hysteria grow later into true obsessionals. Many with truly obsessional symptoms such as washing compulsions, ritualistic touching, arranging of details, etc., who resemble adult obsessionals in every way while they are young, are nevertheless predestined to develop in later life not obsessional neuroses but schizoid and schizophrenic states instead.

A number of assumptions suggest themselves to explain these inconsistencies. Obviously, even where the dominant drive components remain the same, as with the anal sadism of the delinquent and obsessional neurotic, the choice between the two opposite pathological solutions depends on their interaction with the ego attitudes and these alter while maturation and development are ongoing. Death wishes, aggression, dishonesty, which are acceptable to the individual on one ego and superego level, are condemned and defended against on the next; hence the change from delinquent to compulsive traits. Or, again with the maturing of the ego, defenses against anxiety which make use of the motor system such as bodily conversion and phobic retreat change to defense mechanisms within the thought processes such as counting, magical formulas, undoing, isolating; this explains the step from hysterical to obsessional symptomatology. Mixtures of hysterical and obsessional symptoms may have simple explanations: children who produce a permanent hysterical disturbance nevertheless acquire additionally a number of transitory compulsive symptoms while passing through the anal-sadistic stage for which the latter are appropriate; in others, in whom a permanent obsessional neurosis is in the making, free-floating anxieties, phobias, and hysterical symptoms still persist as residues of the developmental level which has gone before. In the youngest obsessionals, the ambivalence conflicts and compulsions have to be understood probably as early ominous signs of splits and disharmonies within the structure, severe enough to lead later to a psychotic total disintegration of the personality.

There is a further finding which every analyst can make in the diagnostic service of a children's clinic, namely, that the field of mental disorders in childhood is more extensive than expected from experience with adult psychopathology. Among the material there is, of course, a nucleus of all the typical forms of compulsions, ceremonials, rituals, anxiety attacks, phobias, traumatically caused and psychosomatic disorders, inhibitions, and character deformations which come under the heading of the infantile neuroses; or the severe withdrawals from the object world and estrangements from reality which come under the heading of the infantile psychoses. But these are by no means the majority. Besides them, there are the (nonorganic) disturbances of vital body needs, i.e., the feeding and sleeping disorders of the infant; the (nonorganic) excessive delays in acquiring vital capacities such as control of motility, speech, cleanliness, learning; the primary disturbances of narcissism[2] and of object relations; the states caused by uncontrolled destructive and self-destructive tendencies, or by uncontrolled derivatives of sex and aggression; the retarded and infantile personalities. Some of these children never reach the phallic-oedipal phase, which is the true starting point for the infantile neurosis. Some have underdeveloped, primitive, and defective defense organizations, with the result that their symptoms correspond to irruptions from the id rather than to compromise formations between id and ego. With some, superego formation is so incomplete that moral judgment, guilt, and internal conflict are lacking as controlling inner forces.

So far, there are only descriptive and not sufficiently detailed dynamic formulations to account for the variety of clinical pictures with which the field is crowded. Perhaps some of the disorders which occur in the first years of life represent prestages of neurotic development to be changed into neuroses proper with the age-adequate increases in ego and superego growth and with the advances in structuralization. Others may represent abortive neuroses, i.e., unsuccessful, incomplete, short-term attempts of the ego agencies to come to terms with and modify the drives.

THE DEVELOPMENTAL DISTURBANCES

As mentioned above, mental disturbances are more frequent in number and more varied in kind in children than they are in adults. Their incidence is increased on the one hand by the circumstances caused by the child's dependence, and

[2] See J. J. Sandler, "Disorders of Narcissism" (a series of papers to be published).

on the other by the strains and stresses of development itself.

External Stresses

Due to their inability to care for themselves, infants and children have to put up with whatever care is given them. Where child management is not extremely sensitive, this causes a number of disturbances, the earliest of which are usually centered around sleep, feeding, elimination, and the wish for company.

In all four areas the child's own natural inclinations are out of harmony with many of the present cultural and social habits. The child has his own *sleep* rhythm, but this rarely coincides with the time of day or night or the length of time the mother wishes him to sleep to fit her own schedule. He has his own methods of making the transition from waking to sleeping by means of autoerotic activities such as thumb sucking, masturbation, or cuddling the transitional objects (Winnicott, 1953), but he can use them freely only with the indulgence of the mother, who often interferes. It is a primitive need of the child to have close and warm skin contact with another person's body while falling asleep, but this runs counter to all the rules of hygiene which demand that children sleep by themselves and not share the parental bed. What *nourishment* children want to take, at what time, and in what amounts, is rarely left to their own choice (except in infant feeding on demand), with the result that painful waiting periods are imposed on their hunger, or food is urged on them when it is not wanted. Except in the most modern types of upbringing, *toilet training* is introduced too early, namely, at a time when neither the child's primitive muscular control nor his personality advances toward body management are ready for it. The infant's biological need for the caretaking adult's constant *presence* is disregarded in our Western culture, and children are exposed to long hours of solitude owing to the misconception that it is healthy for the young to sleep, rest, and later play alone. Such neglect of natural needs creates the first breaks in the smooth functioning of the processes of need and drive fulfillment. As a result, mothers seek advice for infants who have difficulty in falling asleep or do not sleep through the night, in spite of being tired; who do not eat enough or refuse appropriate foods, in spite of their bodies' obvious need for nourishment; or who cry excessively and are unable to accept comfort offered by the mother. So far as disturbances of this order are due to environmental handling, they can be eliminated from the field if different ways of child care are used from the beginning. Once they are produced, however, their consequences cannot be removed altogether, not even if beneficial changes in the form of management are made. The frustrations and unpleasures experienced by the child in connection with a particular need or component drive remain associated with it in his mind. This weakens the effectiveness and positive urgency of the drive, renders it vulnerable, and consequently prepares the way for future neurotic trouble in the afflicted area (see also A. Freud, 1946).

Inconsiderate handling of the infant's early needs has some further repercussions for pathological development. In his growth toward independence and self-reliance, the child accepts the mother's initial gratifying or frustrating attitude as a model which he imitates and recreates in his own ego. Where she understands, respects, and satisfies his wishes as far as possible, there are good chances that his ego will show equal tolerance. Where she unnecessarily delays, denies, and disregards wish fulfillment, his ego is likely to develop more of the so-called "hostility toward the id," i.e., a readiness for internal conflict, which is one of the prerequisites of neurotic development.

Internal Stresses

In contrast to the externally given stresses which, to a large extent, are avoidable, the internal stresses are inevitable. They are more virulent in instances where previous (externally caused) damage has undermined the organic intactness of the drives, and less so where drive activity has remained healthy. But, in essence, they are as inescapable as maturation and development themselves. Unlike the pathological formations of adult life, they are transitory in spite of being intense and are "outgrown" with the passing of the developmental phase in which they have emerged.

DISTURBANCES OF SLEEP

However carefully and successfully an infant's sleeping habits and arrangements have been handled in the first year of life, difficulties with sleep, or with the ease of falling asleep, intervene almost without exception in the second year. A one-year-old, in the absence of any bodily need, pain, or discomfort, may drop off to sleep whenever he is tired, at a moment's notice, sometimes in the middle of play or with a feeding spoon still in his hand. But only a few months later, the same child will protest when put to bed, in spite of tiredness, and will toss and turn, or call out for company for any length of time. The impression is given that he "fights against sleep," sometimes all the more so the greater his exhaustion. What has happened here is that falling asleep is no longer a purely physical affair as the almost automatic response to a body need in an undifferentiated individual, in whom ego and id, self and object world are not yet separated off from each other. With the strengthening of the child's object ties and of his involvement in the happenings of the external world, withdrawal of libido and of ego interests to the self becomes a prerequisite for sleep. This is not always accomplished without difficulty, and the anxiety aroused by the process makes the toddler cling all the more tenaciously to his wakefulness. The symptomatic manifestations of the state are the endless calls from the child's bed, the demands for the mother's presence, for an open door, a drink of water, etc. These again disappear spontaneously when the child's object relationships become more secure and less ambivalent, and when his ego becomes stabilized sufficiently to permit regression to the undifferentiated, narcissistic state necessary for sleep.

As mentioned before, the child's spontaneous methods for facilitating the transition from wakefulness to sleep are the autoerotic activities such as rocking, thumb sucking, masturbation, and the use of transitional objects such as cuddly toys, soft materials, etc. When the latter are given up or when at a later age masturbation is fought against, this frequently causes a new wave of difficulties in falling asleep. If this happens at the latency stage, the new methods used by the child to combat the disturbance are commonly obsessional ones such as counting, compulsive reading, compulsive thinking, etc.

Although the child's difficulties in falling asleep resemble in manifest appearance the sleeping disorders of depressive or melancholic adults, the underlying metapsychological picture is different, and therefore the former state is not to be considered as a forerunner of the latter. What the two have in common is no more than the vulnerability of the area of sleep.

DISORDERS OF FOOD INTAKE

More is known about the child's eating disturbances and food fads, which have a long history and are varied in kind.[3] The various disorders of food intake belong legitimately to the various stages of the developmental line toward independent eating, as they follow each other and are outgrown one after the other.

Chronologically their sequence runs the following approximate course. The first upsets are connected with the establishing of breast feeding and are of mixed causation: from the mother's side there are bodily obstacles regarding the flow of milk and the shape of nipples; psychological ones regarding her ambivalent or anxious response to breast feeding. The child may have organic difficulties such as a delayed sucking response or a lowered urge for food intake; or psychological ones in the form of an automatic negative reaction to the mother's anxiety or hesitation. Next in line are the frequent food refusals at the time of weaning from breast or bottle, although these can be prevented by considerate, very gradual weaning. Where they are excessive, they commonly leave their mark in the form of anger with food, dislike for new tastes and consistencies, lack of adventurousness in eating, lack of pleasure in the oral sphere.

[3] See Chapter 3, "The Developmental Line from Suckling to Rational Eating"; and A. Freud (1946).

Sometimes they leave the opposite result, namely, inordinate greed and the fear of going hungry.

Battles about eating the mother's food express the toddler's ambivalent relationship to her. An excellent clinical illustration of this was a toddler who, when angry with his mother, not only spit out what she fed him, but also scraped his tongue of any morsel of food adhering to it. Literally he "would have none of her." Battles about the amount of food intake alternate with battles about the type of food which is preferred or rejected, i.e., food fads, and those about the mechanics of eating, i.e., table manners. More in the nature of symptoms is the disgusted avoidance of particular shapes, smells, colors, and consistencies of food, an avoidance which is derived from defense against anal trends; or vegetarianism which (if not produced and maintained by environmental influences) results from defense against regressive cannibalistic and sadistic fantasies; or refusal of fattening foods, sometimes of food altogether, in the service of warding off fantasies of oral impregnation or of pregnancy.

Since these various forms of symptomatic behavior are developmental manifestations, each in its own right, there is no need to fear, as parents often do, that the milder forms, such as the food fads, are prestages of the more severe ones, such as far-reaching food refusal, and that the one will change into the other if they are not treated. They are by definition transitory and open to spontaneous cure. Nevertheless, any excessive upset in the eating process on an earlier stage will leave residues which increase and complicate disturbances on the later ones. In general, the eating disturbances of childhood leave the area of food intake vulnerable and this prepares the ground for the neurotic afflictions of stomach and appetite in adult life.

THE ARCHAIC FEARS

Before children develop the anxieties which are coordinate with the increasing structuralization of their personality,[4] they pass through an earlier phase of anxiety which is distressing not only to them but also to the onlooker, due to its intensity. These anxieties are often called "archaic" since their origin cannot be traced to any previous frightening experience but seems to be included in the innate disposition. Descriptively, they are fears of darkness, of loneliness, of strangers, of new and unaccustomed sights and situations, of thunder, sometimes of the wind, etc. Metapsychologically, they are not phobias since, unlike the phobias of the phallic phase, they are not based on regression or conflict or displacement. Instead, they seem to express the immature ego's weakness and paniclike disorientation when faced with unkown impressions which cannot be mastered and assimilated.

The archaic fears disappear in proportion to the developmental increase in the various ego functions such as memory, reality testing, secondary process functioning, intelligence, logic, etc., and especially with the decrease of projection and magical thinking.

THE BEHAVIOR DISORDERS OF THE TODDLER

Behavior difficulties of the toddler cause much concern, especially when they assume proportions which are unmanageable for the mother. The manifestations are tied to the

[4] See Chapter 4, pp. 131-133.

height of anal sadism and express its trends in part directly through destructiveness, messiness, and motor restlessness, and in part reactively, through clinging, inability to separate, whining, unhappiness, chaotic affective states (including temper tantrums).

For all its severity and pathological appearance, the whole syndrome is short-lived. It remains in force while there are no other than motor outlets for the child's drive derivatives and affects, and it disappears or decreases in intensity as soon as new pathways for discharge have been opened up, especially by the acquisition of speech (Anny Katan, 1961).

A TRANSITORY OBSESSIONAL PHASE

Excessive orderliness and cleanliness, ritualistic behavior and bedtime ceremonials, which we are used to associate in our minds with the obsessional neurosis or obsessional character, appear in the majority of children around or after the height of the anal phase. They correspond on the one hand to the defenses set up as a result of toilet training and on the other to specific developmental aspects of the ego which usually, though not invariably, coincide with the problems of anality (H. Hartmann, 1950a). The fact that during this period the child behaves as if obsessional creates a misleading semblance of pathology. In the ordinary course of events the compulsive manifestations disappear without trace as soon as the relevant drive and ego positions have been outgrown.

On the other hand, the normally transitory obsessional manifestations represent a threat of permanent pathology if, for some reason, the libidinal investment in the anal-sadistic phase has been excessive so that large amounts of libido remain fixed to it. In these cases the child will return to anal sadism, usually after some frightening experience on the phallic level. Only such regressions, with the defenses against them and the resultant compromise formations, form the basis of true and lasting obsessional pathology.

DISTURBANCES OF THE PHALLIC PHASE, PREADOLESCENCE AND ADOLESCENCE

The manner in which drive and ego progression either cures or causes the developmental disturbances is displayed most convincingly at those transition points between phases where not only the quality but also the quantity of drive activity undergoes a change. An example is the extreme castration fear, the death fears and wishes, together with the defenses against them, which dominate the scene at the height of the phallic-oedipal phase, and which create the well-known inhibitions, masculine overcompensations, passive and regressive moves of this period. This cluster of symptoms disappears as if by magic as soon as the child takes the first steps into the latency period, that is, as an immediate reaction to the biologically determined lessening of drive activity. Compared with the oedipal child, the latency child seems definitely less beset by problems.

The opposite happens at the transition point from latency to preadolescence. At this time, changes in the quality as well as quantity of the drives and the increase in several primitive pregenital trends (especially oral and anal) cause a severe loss of social adaptation, of sublimations and, in general, of personality gains which have been achieved during the latency period. The impression of health and rationality disappears again and the preadolescent seems to be less mature, less normal, and often appears to have delinquent leanings.

This picture changes once more with the entry into adolescence proper. The emerging genital trends act as a transitory cure for any of the passive-feminine leanings acquired during the negative oedipus complex and carried forward through latency and preadolescence. They also do away with the diffuse pregenitality of preadolescence. Apart from this, as amply described by many authors (e.g., Eissler, 1958; Geleerd, 1958), adolescence produces its own symptomatology which, in the more severe cases, is of a quasi-dissocial, quasi-psychotic, borderline order. This pathology also disappears when adolescence has run its course.[5]

DISSOCIALITY, DELINQUENCY, CRIMINALITY AS DIAGNOSTIC CATEGORIES IN CHILDHOOD

The Age Factor in Social Development, Legal and Psychological

Besides the diagnostic categories discussed in the preceding sections, there are others which either cannot be applied

---

[5] In a paper on "The Infantile Neuroses" (to be published) Dr. H. Nagera makes the useful suggestion that the developmental disturbances should be subdivided as follows:

(a) *developmental disturbances or interferences* defined as instances when external demands are made on the child which are neither reasonable nor age adequate and with which the child's ego cannot cope, or cannot cope without upset and distress;

(b) *developmental conflicts* defined as being experienced by every child to a greater or lesser degree either when certain specific environmental demands are made at appropriate developmental phases or when developmental and maturational levels are reached which create specific conflicts;

(c) *neurotic conflicts* defined as arising between drive activity and internalized demands, i.e., superego precursors;

(d) *infantile neuroses.*

to children without modification or from which certain periods of childhood are exempt altogether. Examples of these are dissociality, delinquency, and criminality.

The uncertainties about their application are reflected clearly on the legal side in the ongoing debates about the age limit below which a child brought before the Court should be classified merely as "out of control," "in need of care and protection";[6] up to which age there should be at least the "presumption of lack of criminal responsibility," which has to be rebutted by evidence all the more strongly the nearer the child is to eight years of age;[7] how long the young person before the Court should be given "benefit of age" when intent is proved.[8] The trend in recommendations now being considered in England and elsewhere is toward raising these ages and especially the age for full responsibility before the law.[9]

As in the law, also in educational and psychoanalytic usage, we find uncertainty about the ages for which the designations of dissocial, delinquent, criminal are appropriate. By rights, we should not apply them to the earliest

[6] In England now, up to the age of eight, before which he is considered incapable of criminal intent and of committing an offense in the technical sense.

[7] In England now, up to fourteen.

[8] In England at present, fourteen to seventeen.

[9] In England it is at present recommended to raise the age for the possibility of criminal intent to twelve, and later to fourteen. In the United States this age limit has already been raised from seven to sixteen, eighteen, and even to twenty-one in some states. On the European continent thirteen or fourteen appears as the average age. Internationally, criminologists have agreed that it is "desirable that the full age for the purposes of the penal law in European countries should not be fixed below 18."

For this and additional information see T. E. James (1962, pp. 124, 125, 129, 158-160). For the corresponding ages in the United States see Neil Peck (1962).

disagreements of young children with their environment, even if these upsets consist of disorderly and disruptive behavior and are extremely disturbing for the family, i.e., for the first social community to which the child belongs. Presumed lack of criminal intent in the legal sense is matched on the psychoanalytic side by the notion that the young child cannot be pronounced to behave either in a "social" or "dissocial" manner before he has at least the ability to perceive and understand the social setting to which he belongs and can identify with the rules that govern it. In agreement with the law we believe that the acquisition of these abilities is a function of increasing age and maturity, although we expect to see them develop earlier, not later than the minimum ages stipulated by the law. Also in agreement with legal procedure, we give the developing individual the "benefit of age" when assessing social adaptation since we regard the latter as a gradual process, bound up with the development of the drives, the ego and superego, and altogether dependent on their course.

But in spite of these theoretical convictions, and wholly in opposition to legal usage, when it comes to clinical and educational practice we cannot help thinking or talking even of under-fives as behaving antisocially, dissocially, etc., or of showing "latent dissociality" (Aichhorn, 1925). Obviously, this practice is based on our assumption that there are certain intermediary levels of social adaptation which the child should reach at certain ages, and that we have the right to become alarmed if no overt evidence in behavior is given of such progress at the appropriate junctures, i.e., if the expected chronology of gradual social development is disrupted.

According to our psychoanalytic conceptions, the final

achievement of social adaptation is the result of a number and variety of developmental advances. To enumerate and examine these in detail is useful, because in this way we create the prerequisites for predicting future massive disturbance at a time when only the merest indications of disharmony, unevenness in growth, or faulty response to the environment are present. This endeavor also disposes effectively of the conception of dissociality as a nosological entity which is based on one specific cause, whether this is thought to be internal (such as "mental deficiency" or "moral insanity") or external (such as broken homes, parental discord, parental neglect, separations, etc.). As we abandon thinking in terms of specific *causes* of dissociality, we become able to think increasingly in terms of successful or unsuccessful *transformations* of the self-indulgent and asocial trends and attitudes which normally are part of the original nature of the child. This helps to construct developmental lines which lead to pathological results, although these are more complex, less well defined, and contain a wider range of possibilities than the lines of normal development, which were laid down tentatively in the previous chapter.

The Newborn as a Law unto Himself

The newborn begins life, not exempt from laws but with his reactions governed by an overriding internal principle according to which he welcomes pleasurable experience, rejects unpleasure, and strives to reduce tension. It is significant for his further development that he can operate this pleasure principle on his own only in so far as gratification of needs and instinctual demands can be provided by his own body, i.e., in the limited area of autoerotic satisfaction. So far as these (rocking, thumb sucking, various forms of masturbation) are concerned, he is, and may remain, a "law unto himself."[10]

The Caretaking Mother as the First External Legislator

Since in all other respects the infant is unable to satisfy his needs by his own actions, the pleasure principle, in spite of being an internal law lodged in the infant himself, has to be implemented from the outside by the caretaking mother who provides or withholds satisfaction. On the strength of this activity she becomes not only the child's first (anaclitic, need-fulfilling) object but also the first external legislator. The first external laws with which she confronts the infant are concerned with the *timing* and *rationing* of his satisfaction. Here, the types of infant care vary widely in the degree to which they either pay attention to the innate laws or do violence to them. Extreme examples of the latter are the regimes in which unpleasure is disregarded and pleasure kept at a minimum in the interest of training and conditioning of the needs (such as the Truby King method); examples of the former are the regimes based on the avowed purpose of following the pleasure principle, i.e., of reducing unpleasure and frustration and of increasing the pleasurable experiences to the limits of the mother's capability (such as feeding on demand).

Newborns and infants have little or no choice whether to give in to or stand up against the handling accorded to their needs. Since they cannot maintain their own existence,

[10] If not interfered with unduly by the environment or, after structuralization, by guilt.

environmental legislation reigns supreme. Nevertheless, the first skirmishes between infant and environment are fought out on this battleground of body care, and both partners form their first impressions of each other. The infant experiences the regime as either a friendly or a hostile force, according to the sensitivity or insensitivity toward the pleasure principle which the mother displays in her arrangements. The mother, on her side, has a first chance to experience the infant either as a compliant, accommodating, "easy" child, or as an unyielding, self-willed, "difficult" one, according to the good or bad grace with which he, perforce, submits to the beneficent or adverse rules and regulations which she imposes on his need satisfactions.

External Control Extended to the Drives

As infancy is outgrown, the discrepancies between internal pleasure principle and external reality extend gradually from the realm of the basic body needs (for food, warmth, sleep, body comfort) to the main drive derivatives (such as the pregenital-sexual, the aggressive-destructive, the egoistic-possessive ones). It is as natural for the young child to seek gratification of all these with urgency, immediacy, and complete self-indulgence as it is inevitable for the adult environment to impose restrictions on satisfaction according to the dictates of reality which include avoidance of danger to the child himself, to other people, to property, or later, transgressions against the common social decencies. Clashes between these internal and external concerns manifest themselves in the form of the numerous acts of disobedience, unruliness, naughtiness, the temper tantrums, etc., of the normal young.

Internalization of External Drive Control

To have the fulfillment of one's drives and wishes, their acceptance and rejection, lodged in external authority equals moral dependency and, as such, is the hallmark of the immature. Almost the whole of personality and character formation, as it is known to us, can be viewed also in terms of remedying this humiliating situation and of acquiring for the mature person the right to judge his own actions. To grow toward such moral independence is not a conflict-free process, of course, but the reverse, namely, the outcome of a dynamic struggle in which the capabilities and energies at the disposal of the individual are ranged on one side or the other. In what follows they are described under different headings according to their either helping or hindering the process of socialization.

THE PRINCIPLES OF MENTAL FUNCTIONING AND THEIR BEARING ON SOCIALIZATION

The pleasure principle in its original form and in its later modification, the reality principle, are both internal laws, each of them valid for specific periods, areas, and concerns of the personality. The pleasure principle, as described above, is a supreme law during infancy. After this period it still continues to rule all functioning which is closely connected with the processes in the id such as unconscious and in a lesser degree conscious fantasy life, night dreaming, and symptom formation in neurotic and psychotic illness. The reality principle governs all normal ego pursuits during later childhood and adulthood. Both principles are psychological conceptions, aimed at characterizing different modes of mental functioning. Primarily they were not intended to imply moral or social value judgments.

On the other hand, their implications for social and moral development are all too obvious to be neglected. Functioning according to the pleasure principle means accepting as the overriding aim immediate and indiscriminate need and drive satisfaction regardless of external conditions; it is therefore synonymous with being oblivious of environmental norms. Functioning according to the reality principle restricts, modifies, and postpones gratification in the interest of safety, i.e., it leaves room for the avoidance of adverse consequences which might arise from clashes with the environment. Therefore, the former is linked as firmly with asocial, dissocial, "irresponsible" behavior as the latter is essential for social adaptation and the development of law-abiding attitudes. Nevertheless, it would be wrong to assume that the relationship between reality principle and socialization is a simple one. August Aichhorn (1925) was the first to point out that delinquents and criminals may reach a high degree of adaptation to reality without placing this capacity in the service of social adaptation. It remains true that social behavior cannot come about unless the individual has progressed from the pleasure principle to the reality principle. But the statement is not reversible in the sense that this advance in itself guarantees socialization.

The child's advance from the pleasure principle to the reality principle implies a growing tolerance for the frustration of drives and wishes, for their postponement in time, for inhibition in their aim, for their displacement onto other aims and objects, for the acceptance of substitute pleasures, all of which are invariably accompanied by a quantitative reduction of wish fulfillment. In fact, this growing frustration tolerance of the child is regarded by many authors as the decisive factor in the process of socialization, its absence or defectiveness as a major reason for dissocial and delinquent behavior. This opinion, though valid within a limited frame of reference, is an oversimplification if applied to the whole process of social development, for which many other elements of equal importance have to be taken into account.

THE DEVELOPMENT OF EGO FUNCTIONS AS A PRECONDITION OF SOCIALIZATION

If the process of socialization of the individual depends to a large extent on the forward move from pleasure to reality principle, the latter in its turn depends on the ego functions which have to develop beyond certain primitive levels to make the advance possible. Sensations and perceptions, for example, have to be collected and stored in the mental apparatus in the form of *memory traces* before the individual can act on experience and foresight, i.e., act in a manner adapted to reality conditions. Sensations arising from the inner world have to be distinguished from perceptions aroused by external stimuli, i.e., *reality* has to be *tested* and separated from the products of fantasy before wish fulfillment by means of hallucination is abandoned in favor of purposeful action. *Speech* and with it the introduction of *reason* and *logic* into the thought processes mean in themselves an enormous advance in socialization. They imply the understanding of *cause* and *effect*, which has been missing before and without which environmental rules were merely confusing to the child, as extraneous influences enforcing mechanical submission. They also introduce trial action in thought, i.e., make it possible for the child to insert reasoning between the arising of an instinctual wish and the behavior aimed at its fulfillment. When the child's *muscular actions* come under the *control* of the sensible ego instead of serving the impulses in the id, this is another important step toward socialization. Finally, there are essential advances in the integrative function of the ego. They synthesize what in infantile life is a bundle of chaotic impulses and attitudes and turn it gradually into a structuralized unit with its own character and personality.

It is this developing of the ego functions beyond the primary process level that is as relevant for socialization as any other developmental advance. We do not expect to find social attitudes in infants in the preverbal era, or before memory, reality testing, secondary thought processes have been established. Equally, we do not expect them from low-grade defectives or other ego-damaged individuals. We also expect that socialization will be undone when severe ego regressions in later life lower the ego functions to the preverbal and primary process levels.

EGO MECHANISMS FURTHERING SOCIALIZATION

The advances described, from pleasure principle to reality principle and from primary to secondary mental functioning, both serve to narrow the gap between internal and external laws; they are unable to close it without the help given by certain ego mechanisms which base their action on the child's libidinal ties to the environment. The most familiar mechanisms acting in this direction are imitation, identification, introjection.

Imitation of parental attitudes is the earliest and most primitive of these, beginning in infancy, and increasing with the growing awareness of the object world.

By imitating the caretaking parents, the infant succeeds in trying himself out in their role of admired and powerful figures who are able to control magically the flow and ebb of need and drive satisfaction, according to rules which, at that stage, are mysterious and alien to the child.

Identification follows these tentative imitations from preoedipal times onward, provided the latter have been pleasurable in result. It is based on the wish to appropriate such desirable aspects permanently by changing the self, or at least the infant's concept of it, in the image of the parents. The parents' own social ideals, whatever they are, are thereby carried from the external into the internal world, where they take root as the child's *ideal self* and become an important forerunner of the superego. To feel at one with the parent in this respect also re-establishes at least on circumscribed moral grounds, the all-over unity between infant and mother (symbiosis) which existed at the beginning of life before any distinctions were made by the child between pleasure-seeking self and pleasure-giving or -withholding object world.

Introjection of external, i.e., parental, authority is added to this new internal agency during and after the oedipal period. It is thereby raised from the status of a mere desirable ideal to that of an effective, actual legislator, i.e., the superego which, from then onward, manages to regulate drive control internally. It does so by rewarding a compliant ego with feelings of well-being and self-esteem and by punishing a rebellious one with pangs of conscience and feelings of guilt, replacing in this way dependence on and fear of the parents, which regulated behavior previously. But even with this measure of internal legislation established, conformity with external authority and active backing by it are still needed by the superego for a lengthy period.

ID ATTRIBUTES AS OBSTACLES TO SOCIALIZATION

The effectiveness of ego growth and of the identificatory and introjective mechanisms may create a false picture, namely, lead us to underestimate the obstacles in the way of socialization with which every immature individual has to cope. The pull toward cathecting, accepting, and internalizing social norms is powerful indeed, owing to the child's libidinal ties to the parents, who are their first representatives. On the other hand, the child's striving toward fulfilling his own instinctual aims is equally imperative. It remains a great hardship for the individual that his sexual and aggressive trends such as they are in infantile life do not fit into the adult cultural norms, that they have to be modified before doing so, and that socialization therefore demands from the child a certain amount of alienation from and turning against what he feels legitimately to be his innermost self.

It has to be granted, on the other side, that some of the necessary modifications are not the effect of conflict and effort but come about more or less spontaneously in the course of natural growth and maturation.

Early cannibalistic fantasies, for example, seem to be dealt with by primary repression before an effective ego or superego are formed. Equally, the indiscriminate aggression and destructiveness of the infant are bound, tamed, and made controllable not by either environmental or internal management but by the spontaneous process of being fused with and brought into the service of the child's libido. Even some of the anal inclinations, toward smell, attraction by excrement and other dirty matter, if not mishandled, overemphasized, and perpetuated by the environment, are almost inevitably displaced and neutralized into culturally acceptable sublimations.

Still, it is vital to note that normally, most other infantile component drives are more persistent and therefore create conflict, initially with the environment, later with the ego agencies so far as these are environmentally oriented. The child then regards the component drives no longer as mere sources of pleasure but scrutinizes them on the basis of their being either suitable or unsuitable, acceptable or unacceptable from the moral and environmental point of view. There is no doubt that greed, demandingness, possessiveness, extreme jealousy and competitiveness, impulses to kill rivals and frustrating figures, i.e., all the normal elements of infantile instinctual life, become nuclei for later dissociality if permitted to remain unmodified and that social growth implies adopting a noncompliant, defensive attitude toward them. As a result of defense on the part of the ego some of them are eliminated from the conscious self altogether (by repression); others are turned into their opposites which are more acceptable (by reaction formation) or deflected to noninstinctual aims (by sublimation); other elements are removed from the context of the self and displaced onto the image of other people (by projection); the more advanced and pleasing phallic components are relegated for fulfillment to a distant future, etc.

The socializing processes, while protecting the child against potentially delinquent tendencies, also restrict, inhibit, and impoverish his original nature. This is not an accidental result, due—as some authors suggest—to the unfortunate use of "pathological" defense mechanisms (such as repression, reaction formation, etc.) instead of "healthy" adaptation "mechanisms" (such as displacement, sublimation); nor is it due to parental emphasis on defense as opposed to a free unfolding of the child's personality. In fact, all defense mechanisms serve simultaneously internal drive restriction and external adaptation, which are merely two sides of the same picture. There is no antithesis between development and defense, since the strengthening of the ego and its defensive organization is itself an essential part of the child's growth and comparable in importance to the unfolding and maturing of the drives. The real antithesis is rooted more deeply and quite inevitably in the aims of development themselves, namely, full individual freedom (implying free drive activity) versus compliance with social norms (implying drive restraint). The difficulty of combining these opposites is rightly regarded as one of the biggest obstacles in the way of successful socialization.[11]

[11] Instead of differentiating between defense and adaptation and labeling the ego mechanisms employed as either pathological or normal, it is preferable to distinguish between their different results; these depend on a variety of factors such as the following:

(a) *Age adequateness*. Defenses have their own chronology, even if only an approximate one. They are more apt to have pathological results if they come into use before the appropriate age or are kept up too long after it. Examples are denial and projection, which are "normal" in early childhood and lead to pathology in later years; or repression and reaction formation, which cripple the child's personality if used too early.

(b) *Balance*. The healthiest defense organization is one where different methods are used for the various danger situations arising from the id and no single mechanism predominates to the exclusion of all others.

(c) *Intensity*. Whether defense leads to symptom formation rather than to healthy social adaptation depends on quantitative factors even more than on qualitative ones. Any overdoing of

Failures of Socialization

The multiplicity of factors involved in the socializing process is matched by the multiplicity of disorders which affect it. As shown in the preceding pages, external management from the side of the parents and internal influences from the side of drive, ego, and superego development make their contributions to the final outcome. The former vary according to cultural, familial, and individual elements; the latter are subject to variations in time as well as to arrests, regressions, and other developmental vicissitudes. Accordingly, the differences between individuals with regard to chronology, consistency, and scope of superego development are considerable and it becomes useful to think in terms of variations of superego formation rather than in terms of deviations from a hypothetically fixed norm.

By now, many factors and constellations are recognized as leading to later dissociality and have been treated as such in the literature. That *failure in higher ego development*, for the reasons given above, results in faulty socialization is borne out by the large number of delinquents and criminals who, on psychological examination, are found to be of primitive, infantile mentality, retarded, deficient, defective, with low intelligence quotients.[12] That *dissociality and criminality* on the part *of the parents* are incorporated into the child's superego by means of normal identification with them has been stressed by many authors (Aich-

---

drive restraint, regardless of the mechanism used, inevitably leads to neurotic results.

(d) *Reversibility.* Defensive activity instigated to ward off dangers in the past should not be kept up in the present when the danger may have become nonexistent.

[12] See J. J. Michaels (1955) on the impulsive delinquent character.

horn, 1925; Augusta Bonnard, 1950). That severe disturbances of socialization arise when *identification* with the
parents is *disrupted* through separations, rejections, and
other interferences with the emotional tie to them has been
emphasized first by August Aichhorn (1925), abundantly
proved by John Bowlby (1944), and has been generally
accepted as established fact.

On the whole, the qualitative factors in the child's
struggle for socialization receive more attention than the
quantitative ones, although the latter are no less responsible
for the number of social breakdowns which occur in childhood. Any alteration in strength on the side of either the
id or ego agencies may overthrow the precarious social
balance of the child. If his ego is weakened for any reason,
he will be unable to control normal drive activity in an age-
adequate manner, will regress to pleasure-seeking, self-indulgent attitudes of earlier times, i.e., become dissocial in
behavior. If there is a quantitative increase in drive activity
in general or in any specific drive component in particular,
his normal ego efforts and defenses will be ineffective in
controlling them. On the other hand, such quantitative
alterations are the order of the day and very much part of
normal life whatever their results. A child's ego is weakened
by physical pain, by illness, by anxiety, by upsetting events,
by any emotional strain, etc. Changes in drive intensity are
also brought about either environmentally through seduction, exposure to observations, excessive indulgence or frustration, or internally by transitions from one developmental
level to another.[13] While these quantitative factors are in

---

[13] Compare, for example, the amount of drive activity during
latency with the periods before and after it. The drop in pressure
from the drives at this time corresponds to the high level of social
responses during latency.

constant flux, no social attitude adopted by the child should be taken as the final one.

When following the literature on the subject we find that it is usually not the components of infantile sexuality but of infantile aggression which are regarded as a threat to socialization. Although convincing on the surface, this view does not stand up to closer examination. In fact, the aggressive strivings, if fused in the normal way with the libidinal ones, are socializing influences, rather than the opposite. They provide the initial strength and tenacity with which the infant reaches out for the object world and holds on to it. In the further course they underlie the ambition to appropriate the parents' qualities and powers as well as the wish to be big and independent. Further, they lend moral strength and severity to the superego in its dealings with the ego when they are deflected from the objects and placed at its disposal.

Aggression becomes a menace to social adaptation only when it appears in pure culture, either unfused with libido or defused from it. The cause of this usually lies not in the aggressive drive itself but in the libidinal processes which may not have developed sufficiently for the task of toning down and binding aggression or which lose that capacity at some point during the child's development owing to disappointments in object love, imagined or real rejections, object loss, etc. A special danger point for defusion is the anal-sadistic phase during which aggression reaches a normal peak and its social usefulness is especially dependent on its close association with equal amounts of libido. Any emotional upset at this time frees the child's normal sadism of its libidinal admixtures so that it becomes pure destructiveness and, as such, turns against animate and inanimate objects as well as against the self. What happens then is that the half-playful, provoking, self-willed attitudes of the toddler become fixed in the personality as quarrelsomeness, ruthless acquisitiveness, and a preference for hostile rather than friendly relations with fellow beings. More important still, aggression in this defused form is not controllable, either externally by the parents or internally by ego and superego. If fusion is not re-established through strengthening of the libidinal processes and new object attachments, the destructive tendencies become a major cause for delinquency and criminality.

Moving from Family to Community Standards

The processes of imitation, identification, and introjection which take place before, during, and after the oedipus complex can take the child no further than the internalization of parental standards. Although these processes are indispensable as a preparatory step for future adaptation to a community of adults, they give no assurance in themselves that this adaptation will finally be achieved, not even in those fortunate instances where family and community standards coincide.

The moral norms on which family life is based are acceptable to the child on two accounts. On the one hand, they are represented by the figures of the parents whom the child loves and with whose attitudes he can identify; on the other hand, they are presented to him in a highly personal manner by parents who are narcissistically identified with him, have sympathy for his peculiarities, and instinctive empathy with his difficulties and idiosyncrasies. Their own emotional involvement with the child prevents them from imposing demands which are beyond the child's horizon of understanding or clearly beyond his capacity of complying with them. In this manner, in the home, the individual child is given not only "benefit of age," but also the benefits of his specific personality and his specific position in the family. It is true that this state of affairs may turn into a handicap, since it leads the child to expect as his right that similar tolerance will be shown to him in later life; but it is also true that the immature ego agencies need this leniency to initiate and increase their positive, receptive attitude to the environment.

However this may be, the child retains only a few of these initial privileges when he moves from home to school. School rules still have a personal flavor in so far as they are represented by the image of the teacher whom, under favorable conditions, the child likes, or loves, or admires, and uses accordingly as an object for identification. On the other hand, school rules take less or no notice of individual differences. Children are graded according to maturity in the sense that different standards are applied to different age groups, but within the age group all individuals are expected to conform to a common norm, whatever sacrifice this may mean to their personalities. For this reason many children find it difficult to achieve the transition from home to school standards. That they have successfully identified and complied with the former is in itself no guarantee that they will successfully identify and comply with the latter. The well-adjusted family child is not necessarily a well-adjusted school child or vice versa.

With the further move of the adolescent from school to the adult community, the legal norms finally become impersonal. To be "equal before the law" is not only an advantage for the individual, it also implies that all claims for benefits, privileges, preferential treatment on personal grounds have to be abandoned. It remains a difficult step, and one not achieved by everybody, to accept that the community enforces its laws, and punishes transgressions, irrespective of the sacrifice in pleasure this means for the individual, without regard for his personal needs, wishes, complexities, and without reference to his intellectual and characterological status which either fits him or incapacitates him for compliance with the law. So far, the only full exceptions granted from the latter are two extreme cases, namely, the moron and the insane, on the basis of their alleged inability to distinguish between right and wrong.

Apart from the basic moral rules which are incorporated in the superego, legal codes in their impersonal, complex, and formal nature do not become part of an individual's internal world. What a functioning superego is expected to ensure is not the individual's identification with the content of any specific laws but his acceptance and internalization of the existence of a governing norm in general. In this respect, the normal citizen in his attitude to the law perpetuates the infantile position of an ignorant and compliant child faced by parents who are omniscient and omnipotent. The delinquent or criminal perpetuates the attitude of the child who ignores, or belittles, or disregards parental authority and acts in defiance of it.

There are also some exceptional individuals whose moral demands on themselves are higher and stricter than anything which the environment expects from them or would impose on them. They acquire their standards by identification with an ideal image of the parents rather than by identifying with the real persons of the parents and they enforce them via a superego which is excessively severe owing to the turning inward of almost all the available aggression. Such individuals feel secure in the internal judgment and regulation of their own behavior which they know to be above and beyond the common norm. In the indirect, circuitous way of extreme (and often obsessional) character development they have succeeded in becoming once more what individuals set out to be as infants, namely, a "law unto themselves."

HOMOSEXUALITY AS A DIAGNOSTIC CATEGORY IN CHILDHOOD DISORDERS

Some of the arguments which apply to dissociality can be used with some alterations in the case of homosexual manifestations in childhood. There is a similar uncertainty regarding the age at which the term homosexuality can legitimately be used. There are similar links between the manifestations of homosexuality and normal developmental stages. There is also a similar difficulty in predicting adult homosexuality proper, i.e., in establishing reliable connections between certain preliminary stages which are visible in childhood and the final abnormal sexual outcome.

Since the publication of the *Three Essays on Sexuality* in 1905, an increasing psychoanalytic literature has concerned itself with the phenomenon of homosexuality from a variety of angles. Not all of the latter are relevant for childhood. The important distinction between manifest and latent homosexuality, for instance, applies to the sexual behavior of adults and cannot be maintained in the same manner when applied to mutual masturbation and other sex play between children or even adolescents. The distinction between passive and active homosexuality, or rather between passive and active underlying fantasies, refers to the positions of the partners in the sexual act itself, i.e., again to practices after adolescence. The whole extensive debate concerning reversibility also applies only to the adult for whom his homosexual way of life is either ego dystonic, and therefore accessible to analysis, or ego syntonic, when treatment is avoided or sought only under external pressure.

On the other hand, there are a number of questions concerning homosexuality which are equally prominent in the literature and which are of great relevance for the child analyst in the sense that he can extract clues from them for his assessments or contribute data to their solution from his own findings. These questions deal with three subjects: with the topic of *object choice*; with the *reconstructions* in adult analysis and their significance for the prognosis of homosexuality in childhood assessments; and with the general question of *causation* of homosexuality by weighing inborn against acquired elements.

Object Choice: The Age Factor

That children of both sexes make libidinal attachments to love objects of both sexes is one of the basic propositions in the psychoanalytic theory of infantile sexuality. In each period of childhood object choice is governed by different rules, needs, and necessities, as descriptions which follow will show. Thus, ties to persons of the same sex are as normal as ties to the opposite sex and they cannot be considered as forerunners of later homosexuality.[14]

Infants, at the beginning of life, choose their objects on the basis of function, not of sex. The mother is cathected with libido because she is the caretaking, need-fulfilling provider, the father as a symbol of power, protectiveness, ownership of the mother, etc. A "mother relationship" is often made to the male parent in cases where he takes over the need-fulfilling role, or a "father relationship" to the female parent in cases where she is the dominant power in the family. In this manner, the normal infant, whether male or female, has object attachments to both, male and female figures. Although in the strict sense of the term the infant is neither heterosexual nor homosexual, he can also be described as being both.

That the object's functions and not sex decide these relationships is borne out also by the transference in analytic treatment, where the sex of the analyst is no barrier against both mother and father relationships being displaced onto him.

Apart from this object choice of the anaclitic type, however, it is obvious that the *pregenital component trends* depend for their satisfactions not on the sexual apparatus of the partner but on other qualities and attitudes. If these are found in the mother and if on the strength of them she becomes the child's main love object, then the boy in the

---

[14] "On the contrary, psycho-analysis considers that a choice of an object independently of its sex—freedom to range equally over male and female objects—as it is found in childhood, in primitive states of society and early periods of history, is the original basis from which, as a result of restriction in one direction or the other, both the normal and the inverted types develop" (S. Freud, 1905, p. 145f.; footnote added in 1915).

oral and anal phases is "heterosexual," the girl "homosexual"; if they are found in the father instead of in the
mother, the position is reversed. In either case, a choice
of object determined by the quality and aim of the dominant drive component is phase adequate and normal, irrespective of whether the resulting partnership is a heterosexual or homosexual one.

In contrast to the preceding stages, the sex of the object
becomes of great importance in the *phallic phase*. The
phase-adequate overestimation of the penis induces both
boys and girls to choose partners who possess a penis, or at
least are believed to do so (such as the phallic mother).
Whatever course their instinctive trends have taken otherwise, they cannot disengage themselves "from a class of
objects defined by a particular determinant."[15]

The oedipus complex itself, both in its positive and negative form, is based on the recognition of sex differences, and
within its framework the child makes his object choice in
the adult manner on the basis of the partner's sex. The
positive oedipus complex with the parent of the opposite
sex as preferred love object corresponds as closely to adult
heterosexuality as the negative oedipus complex with the
tie to the parent of the same sex corresponds to adult
homosexuality. So far as both manifestations are normal
developmental occurrences, they are inconclusive for later
pathology; they merely fulfill legitimate bisexual needs of

[15] ". . . like little Hans, who showed his affection to little boys
and girls indiscriminately, and once described his friend Fritzl as
'the girl he was fondest of'. Hans was a homosexual (as all children
may very well be), quite consistently with the fact, which must
always be kept in mind, that *he was acquainted with only one kind
of sexual organ*—a genital organ like his own" (S. Freud, 1909,
p. 110).

the child. Nevertheless, in the individual child the emphasis may be either on the positive or on the negative oedipal attitudes and these quantitative differences can be taken as prognostic indicators for the future. They reveal important preferences for either one or the other sex which are rooted in preoedipal experiences. On the one hand, the personalities of the parents and their own success or failure in their sexual roles have left their mark via the identifications, which have followed object love. On the other hand, the fixations to aggressive-sadistic trends push the boy as firmly in the direction of the positive oedipus complex and later heterosexuality as the fixations to the passive oral and anal strivings force him toward the negative oedipus complex and, perhaps, later homosexuality.

Altogether, the child's behavior during the phallic oedipal period foreshadows more closely than at other times his future inclinations regarding sexual role and choice of sexual object.

When entry into the *latency period* is made, this particular aspect of the child's libidinal life disappears once more from view. There are, of course, at this time, unmodified remnants of the oedipus complex which determine the attachments, particularly of the neurotic children, who have been unable to solve, and dissolve, their oedipal relationships to the parents. But apart from these, there are also the phase-adequate aim-inhibited, displaced or sublimated tendencies for which the sexual identity of the partner becomes again a matter of comparative indifference. Evidence of the latter are the latency child's relationships to his teachers, who are loved, admired, disliked, or rejected not because they are men or women but because they are either helpful, appreciative, inspiring, or harsh, intolerant, anxiety-arousing figures.

The diagnostician's assessments at this period are further confused by the fact that object choice with regard to contemporaries proceeds on lines opposite to those usual in the adult. The boy who looks for exclusively male companionship and avoids and despises girls is not the future homosexual, whatever the similarity in manifest behavior. On the contrary, such clinging to the males and retreat from and contempt for the females can be considered as the hallmark of the normal masculine latency boy, i.e., the future heterosexual. At this age the future homosexual tendencies are betrayed, rather, by a preference for play with girls and appreciation and appropriation of their toys. This reversal of behavior is taken for granted in latency girls, who seek boyish company not if they are feminine but if they are "tomboys" themselves, i.e., on the basis of their penis envy and masculine wishes, not on the basis of feminine desires for relations with the opposite sex. What appears in overt behavior as homosexual leanings are, in fact, heterosexual ones and vice versa. What has to be remembered in this connection is that the choice of playmates in the latency period (i.e., object choice among contemporaries) is based on identification with the partner, not on object love proper, that is, on equality with them, which may or may not include equality of sex.

In *preadolescence* and in *adolescence*, finally, homosexual episodes are known to occur more or less regularly and to exist side by side with heterosexual ones without being in themselves reliable prognostic signs. These manifestations have to be understood in part as recurrences of the young child's pregenital, sexually indiscriminate object ties, which become valid once more in preadolescence together with the revival of many other pregenital and preoedipal attitudes. Homosexual object choice in adolescence is due also to the adolescent's regression from object cathexis to love for his own person and identification with the object. In this latter respect the adolescent's object represents in many cases not only the individual's real self, but his ideal of himself, a concept which invariably includes the adolescent's ideal notion of his sexual role. Adolescent partnerships formed on these grounds display all the outward signs of homosexual object love and are frequently accepted as true prestages of adult homosexuality. But metapsychologically they are narcissistic phenomena which as such belong to the varied schizoid symptomatology of adolescence, and they are more significant as pointers to the depth of regression than as prognostic indicators for the individual's future sexual role.

Prognosis versus Reconstruction

Compared with the small number of prognostic clues to be found when following the forward movement of the child's libido, there is a mass of relevant data reconstructed in the analysis of adult homosexuals which trace back the various manifestations of latent and overt homosexuality to their infantile roots. In the relevant literature the origin of homosexuality is discussed with regard to the following areas of personality development, periods, and experiences:

the individual's inborn endowment, i.e., bisexuality as the instinctual basis of homosexuality (Freud, 1905, especially footnote added in 1915, 1909; Böhm, 1920; Sadger, 1921; Bryan, 1930; Nunberg, 1947; Gillespie, 1964);

the individual's narcissism which creates the need to choose a sexual partner in the image of himself (Ferenczi, 1911, 1914; Freud, 1914; Böhm, 1933);

the links of homosexuality with the oral and anal pregenital phases (Böhm, 1933; Grete Bibring, 1940; Sadger, 1921; Lewin, 1933);

the overestimation of the penis in the phallic phase (Freud, 1909; Sadger, 1920; Jones, 1932; Lewin, 1933; Loewenstein, 1935; Fenichel, 1936; Pasche, 1964);

the influence of excessive love for and dependence on either mother or father or extreme hostility to either of them (Freud, 1905, 1918, 1922; Sadger, 1921; Weiss, 1925; Böhm, 1930, 1933; Wulff, 1941);

traumatic observations of the female genitalia and of menstruation (Daly, 1928, 1943; Nunberg, 1947);

envy of the mother's body (Böhm, 1930; Melanie Klein, 1957);

jealousy of rival brothers who are subsequently turned into love objects (Freud, 1922; Lagache, 1950); etc.

Notwithstanding such numerous and well-documented links between infantile past and adult present, the reasoning cannot be reversed and the reconstructed data cannot be used for the early spotting of homosexual development in children. The reason why this cannot be done becomes obvious whenever one of the homosexual types is examined in detail, such as, for example, the passive feminine male homosexual whose psychopathology has been particularly closely studied in many therapeutic analyses.

This type of homosexuality is characterized by being mother bound, unwilling and unable to carry out sexual intercourse with women, and by sexual activity with men, usually of a socially inferior order, who are sought out because they possess crudely masculine bodily attributes such as great muscular strength, a hairy body, etc. When analyzed, this homosexual symptomatology can be traced back to a passionate attachment to the mother which dominated infancy and childhood, from the oral through the anal and beyond the phallic phase; to a horror of the female body, usually acquired traumatically after discovering the mother's or a sister's genitals; and to a period of fascinated admiration of the father's penis.

These elements, which undoubtedly are pathogenic influences in the past of the homosexual, can nevertheless not be used for the prognosis of homosexuality if they form part of the clinical picture of a child. Far from being abnormal or even unusual manifestations, they are, on the contrary, regular and indispensable parts of every boy's developmental equipment. The close tie to the mother, which devastates the future homosexual by increasing his fear of the rival father, by heightening his castration anxiety, and by enforcing his regression to anal and oral dependency, is also the well-known centerpiece of the positive oedipus complex and as such the normal prestage of adult heterosexuality. The shock which every boy experiences when he is confronted with the female genital for the first time, and which creates in the later homosexual a lasting aversion against any attractions by the female sex, is a usual event and unavoidable since he begins by believing that every human being has a penis like himself. Normally, the discovery of the difference between the sexes means no more to the boy than a temporary increase in castration anxiety; it may even act as a healthy strengthening of his defenses against his own feminine wishes and identifications, may reinforce his pride in his own possession of a penis and merely give rise to the pitying contempt for the castrated female, which is a truly masculine characteristic of the phallic boy. Finally, the admiration for the bigger man's penis, which dominates the love life of this type of passive homosexual to the exclusion of all else, is also a normal intermediary station in every boy's relationship to his father. The future homosexual remains fixed here and continues to endow his male objects with all the desirable signs of masculine strength and potency, while the normal boy outgrows the stage, identifies with the father as the possessor of the penis, and acquires his male characteristics and heterosexual attitudes for his own person and future sexual identity.

In other words, that certain childhood elements in given cases have led to a specific homosexual result does not exclude a different or even the opposite outcome in other instances. Obviously, what determines the direction of development are not the major infantile events and constellations in themselves but a multitude of accompanying circumstances, the consequences of which are difficult to judge both retrospectively in adult analysis and prognostically in the assessment of children. They include external and internal, qualitative and quantitative factors. Whether a boy's love for his mother is a first step on his road to manhood or whether it will cause him to repress his aggressive masculinity for her sake, depends not only on himself, i.e., on the healthy nature of his phallic strivings, the intensity of his castration fears and wishes, and on the amounts of libido left behind at earlier fixation points. The outcome also depends on the mother's personality and her actions, on the amounts of satisfaction and frustration which she administers to him orally and anally, during feeding and toilet training, on her own wish to keep him dependent on her, or her own pride in his achieving independence of her, and, last but not least, on her acceptance or rejection of pleasure in or intolerance for his phallic advances toward her. The castration shocks which no boy can escape, whether in the shape of threats, observations, operations, etc., depend primarily, as far as the intensity of their consequences is concerned, on the time when they occur and make themselves felt most when they coincide with the height of phallic masturbation, passive-feminine wishes toward the father, guilt feelings, etc. The castration fears and passive strivings in their turn are influenced by the father's repressive or seductive attitudes, his suitability or unsuitability for the role of masculine model, etc. Where the father is absent owing to divorce, desertion, death, there is the lack of a restraining oedipal rival, a circumstance which intensifies anxiety and guilt in the phallic phase and promotes unmanliness. In this situation, the boy's fantasy that the father has been removed by the mother as a punishment for his masculine aggression also acts as a disturbance to the boy's normal heterosexual wishes.

What has to be reckoned with, finally, and what may encourage development in one or the other sexual direction are the purely chance happenings such as accidents, seductions, illnesses, object losses through death, the ease or difficulty of finding a heterosexual object in adolescence, etc. Since such events are unpredictable and may alter the child's life at any date, they upset whatever prognostic calculations may have been made previously.

Homosexuality, Favored or Prevented by Normal Developmental Positions

According to the previous arguments it seems preferable to think not in terms of infantile prestages of adult homosexuality but in terms of developmental influences which

promote or prevent homosexual development. Such thinking is based on the assumption that during the child's
growth homosexual leanings compete and regularly alternate with normal heterosexuality and that the two tendencies make use in turn of the various libidinal positions
through which the child passes.

Considered from this point of view, homosexual development can be summed up as being favored by the following
factors:

(1) the bisexual tendencies which are considered as part
    of the inborn constitution. They endow all individuals
    with psychological characteristics not only of their own
    but also of the opposite sex and enable them to take as
    love objects, or offer themselves as love objects, not only
    to the opposite but also to their own sex. This innate
    bisexuality is intensified in the preoedipal period by the
    identifications with both male and female parent and
    remains the constitutional basis for any homosexual in-
    clinations which arise later.
(2) the individual's primary and secondary narcissism, i.e.,
    the libidinal cathexis of his own self. So far as object
    choice in later childhood follows this original narcis-
    sistic pattern, partners are chosen to be as identical as
    possible with the self, including identity of sex. Such
    homosexual, or more strictly speaking narcissistic rela-
    tionships are characteristic of the latency period and
    certain stages of preadolescence and adolescence.
(3) the anaclitic object attachment of the infant, for which
    sex is of secondary importance. This is of special sig-
    nificance for female homosexuality since the girl may
    become fixated to this stage as to a "homosexual" one.
(4) the libidinization of the anus and the usual passive

tendencies of the anal stage which provide the normal bodily basis for the boy's feminine identification.

(5) penis envy which provides the normal basis for the girl's masculine identification.

(6) the overestimation of the penis in the phallic phase which makes it difficult or impossible for the boy to accept a "castrated" love object.

(7) the negative oedipus complex which represents a normal "homosexual" phase in the life of both boys and girls.

In contrast to the factors enumerated above which urge an individual toward homosexuality, there are other influences at work which act in the opposite direction and protect a given person from adopting this particular sexual solution:

(1) Heterosexual and homosexual strivings compete with each other quantitatively during the whole of childhood. Whatever promotes heterosexuality checks homosexuality to a corresponding degree. For example, the increase in heterosexuality which is bound up with a boy's entry into the phallic phase and the positive oedipus complex automatically decreases any homosexual inclinations which are left over as residues from the period of anal passivity. The same decrease of homosexuality occurs in certain adolescent stages owing to the influx of genital masculinity which turns the boy toward heterosexual object choice.

(2) The very intensity of castration fear which causes some males to avoid women and to become homosexual acts in others as a counterforce against the negative oedipus complex and a barrier against homosexuality. Since the passive feminine wishes toward the father presuppose for their fulfillment the acceptance of castration, they

are avoided by such boys at all costs. This often results in a pseudo masculinity, which is overemphasized as a reaction against castration anxiety, and in a sexual aggressiveness toward women, which denies the possibility of castration and the presence of any feminine wishes and consequently blocks the road to any overt homosexual manifestations.

(3) While undefended regression to anality promotes passive feminine homosexual attitudes in the male, the reaction formations against anality, especially disgust, effectively block the path to homosexuality, or at least to its manifest expression. In adult analysis such men appear as "homosexuals manqués."

(4) Finally, the "tendency to complete development" and the "biological reasonableness" (Edward Bibring, 1936) which make individuals prefer normality to abnormality can be counted as factors weighing against homosexuality.

On the whole, the balance between heterosexuality and homosexuality during the whole period of childhood is so precarious, and the scales are so readily tipped in one direction or the other by a multitude of influences, that the opinion still holds good that "a person's final sexual attitude is not decided until after puberty" (S. Freud, 1905, p. 146; footnote added in 1915).

OTHER PERVERSIONS AND ADDICTIONS AS DIAGNOSTIC CATEGORIES IN CHILDHOOD

Other diagnostic categories which cannot be used outright for children are perversions such as transvestitism, fetishism, addictions.

In these as in the case of all *perversions*, the reason is an obvious one. Since infantile sexuality as such is by definition polymorphously perverse, to label specific aspects of it as perverse is at best an imprecise usage of the term, if it does not imply a total misunderstanding of the· development of the sex instinct. Instead of assessing certain childhood phenomena as perverse, as even analysts are apt to do, the diagnostic questions must be reformulated for these cases and we must inquire which component trends, or under which conditions part of the component trends, are likely to outlast childhood, i.e., when they have to be considered as true forerunners of adult perversion proper.

With regard to manifest behavior some clinical pictures in children are almost identical with those in adult perverts. Nevertheless, this overt similarity need not imply a corresponding metapsychological identity. With adults, the diagnosis of perversion signifies that primacy of the genitals has never been established or has not been maintained, i.e., that in the sexual act itself the pregenital components have not been reduced to the role of merely introductory or contributory factors. Such a definition is necessarily invalid if applied before maturity, i.e., at an age when intercourse does not come into question and while equality of the pregenital zones with the genitals themselves is taken for granted. Accordingly, individuals under the age of adolescence are not perverts in the adult sense of the term, and different viewpoints have to be introduced to account for their relevant symptomatology.

Clinical experience suggests that this symptomatology may be explained by deviations from the developmental norm in two main directions, namely, chronologically and quantitatively.

Chronology is disturbed whenever the specific areas of the body which provide erotic stimulation do not function within the temporal order which corresponds to the normal sequence of libidinal development. Quite apart from the well-known occurrence of later regressions, any one of them may be unusually persistent in its role of providing pleasure, and not fade out in favor of the zones which are next in line according to the laws of maturation. In this respect, the child's *skin erotism* is an instructive illustration. At the beginning of life, being stroked, cuddled, and soothed by touch libidinizes the various parts of the child's body, helps to build up a healthy body image and body ego, increases its cathexis with narcissistic libido, and simultaneously promotes the development of object love by cementing the bond between child and mother. There is no doubt that, at this period, the surface of the skin in its role as erotogenic zone fulfills a multiple function in the child's growth.

On the other hand, these functions become redundant, normally, after infancy. Skin erotism changes its aspect if its gratification remains a major concern of the child after the anal and phallic stages have been reached. Then the skin may continue to be the source of erotic stimulation, while the discharge phenomena for sex excitement have altered developmentally and reached different levels. A boy in the oedipal phase, for example, may crave for skin contact with his mother but, if gratified in reality or fantasy, discharge his excitation in phallic masturbation, similar to an adult pervert who discharges excitement from extragenital sources through the channel of genital orgasm. It is precisely this discrepancy between source of stimulation and outlet for excitation which creates the semblance of perversion in certain childhood cases.[16]

As regards the *quantitative aspect*, i.e., deviations from normal intensities of the component drives, this is obviously a common "variation of normality" within the framework of the child's polymorphously perverse nature. At any time during childhood, any one of the component trends of infantile sexuality or any part aspect of infantile aggression may be unusual in strength and dominate the picture excessively or exclusively. This may be a matter of the inborn constitution. Clinical experience shows, for example, that unusually strong oral strivings are often found in the children of addicts, alcoholics, or manic-depressives. It is also known that the children of obsessional parents show excessively strong anal tendencies, although in these cases whatever is inborn is invariably reinforced by the manner in which obsessional adults handle a child's training for anal cleanliness. Of course, increases in the strength of a component drive may also be due exclusively to environmental influences such as general mismanagement by the parents, seduction, failure of control and guidance, etc. Most frequently the reason for overintensification of a component drive lies in the interaction of external factors with such internal ones as the relative weakness of ego or superego in their dealings with the drives; or, conversely, with excessive superego severity which expresses itself in the overdoing of defense activity. A common example of the last-named

[16] This state of affairs was illustrated very clearly in the analysis of a boy treated by Isabel Paret in the Hampstead Child-Therapy Clinic from age two and a half to four and a half years. In his case it was possible to trace the part played in the child's craving to be stroked to a seductive environmental influence, i.e., to his mother's own addiction to this particular body contact with her child.

constellation are the phallic boys who live in dread of their insufficiently repressed passive-feminine strivings. To ward off castration fears which, in their case, are heightened by castration wishes, they overemphasize overtly all the opposite tendencies with the result that they appear aggressively manly and frequently take on the behavior of phallic *exhibitionists*. Nevertheless, in spite of this behavioral identity, the important difference remains that their type of exhibitionism is an ego device serving the purposes of reassurance and defense, while the adult type is a genuine part of the pervert's drive activity aimed at procuring sexual satisfaction.

Addiction

In the addictions, too, it is the quantitative increase in otherwise normal tendencies which is responsible for creating the impression of "perverse" behavior. Children are often found to be inordinately fond of sweets, apparently in the same manner in which adults are addicted to alcohol or drugs. They feel an overwhelming craving for sweets, use the satisfaction of the craving as an antidote against anxiety, deprivation, frustration, depression, etc., as adults do, and, also as adults do, will go to any length, i.e., lie or steal, to secure possession of the desired substance. But for all this similarity, the metapsychological constellation underlying the manifestation is different in the two instances. The child's love for sweets is a comparatively simple, straightforward expression of a component drive. It has its root in unsatisfied or in overstimulated desires of the oral phase, desires which have grown excessive and by virtue of quantity dominate his libidinal expressions. In later life, these wishes are usually displaced from sweets to other more or less harmless media. They find outlet in some instances in excessive water drinking; in other cases in overeating, in gluttony, perhaps in smoking. On the libidinal side they are expressed in the preference for object relationships of a particular sustaining, comfort-giving type. None of these manifestations by themselves fall into the category of addiction. A true addiction in the adult sense of the term is a more complex structure in which the action of passive-feminine and self-destructive tendencies is added to the oral wishes. For the adult addict the craved-for substance represents not only an object or matter which is good, helpful, and strengthening, as the sweet is for the child, but one which is simultaneously also felt to be injurious, overpowering, weakening, emasculating, castrating, as excessive alcohol or drugs actually are. It is the blending of the two opposing drives, of the desire for strength and weakness, activity and passivity, masculinity and femininity which ties the adult addict to the object of his habit in a manner which has no parallel with what happens in the more benign and positively directed craving of the child.

Transvestitism

Libido-economic factors also play their part in distorting and exaggerating certain other inclinations which are common to all children and in creating thereby the phenomenon of transvestitism as it is not infrequently found in childhood. Here, the increases in strength refer either to the masculine or to the feminine side of the child's nature.

An interest in clothes which are appropriate for the opposite sex or for adults of either sex is as such a common feature of childhood. The popular game of "dressing up" gives children the opportunity of imagining themselves in the role of father or mother, brother or sister, or of carrying out in play any of the occupations which symbolize the parents' roles for them. An umbrella, walking stick, or hat belonging to the father is sufficient to transform the child into the person of the father, a handbag, shoes, or the use of lipstick into the person of the mother. Space-men's or pilots' helmets, bus drivers' caps, red Indians' outfits, nurses' uniforms, etc., are conventional toys designed to create the illusion for the child that he can exchange his own personality for these admired ones via appropriating the necessary clothing. Sex differences are easily transgressed in these fantasy games, especially by girls, and the articles of clothing selected for dressing up are status symbols as frequently as they are sex symbols.

Outside the area of play, with girls in the phase of penis envy, a preference for trousers and other boyish clothing is so familiar that it has come to be considered as age adequate. It does not give rise to concern except in instances where the girl absolutely refuses, and in fact becomes unable to accept, feminine dresses whatever the occasion; then it is taken as a sign that her penis envy, her masculine strivings, and her rejection of her own femininity have reached an unusual height. But even in these extreme cases, it would be a mistake to view the symptomatic expression as parallel in meaning to that of the adult female transvestite. The behavior of such girls is not a sexual manifestation proper, i.e., it is not accompanied by masturbation or masturbation fantasies, nor is it in other ways aimed at providing direct sexual excitation. Instead it serves the purposes of imitation and identification with boys to the extent of actually assuming their role in everyday behavior; of defense against envy and rivalry, against the self-deprecation of feeling castrated, and against the guilt for having caused the alleged self-damage by masturbation. In this manner the "transvestitism" of the phallic girl is as much a function of her defense system as it is an outlet for the masculine side of her innate bisexuality.

There is no complete parallel to this behavior of girls on the boys' side. Apparently, under our cultural conditions, no developmental phase as such normally gives boys the wish to dress as girls. In the isolated cases where such behavior occurs, it impresses one as much more abnormal and usually upsets the parents as an ominous early sign of later sexual aberration.

In a small collection of cases of this kind,[17] the clinical picture can be shown to be fairly uniform. With the symptom proper setting in between the ages of three and five, the boy's accompanying feminine behavior ranges from the mere expression of the wish to be a girl, the desire to be called by a girl's name, playing with girls and their dolls, giving girl's names to the teddy bear, etc., to the actual dressing up in the mother's, a sister's, a favorite nursemaid's underclothes or clothes, with special preference for pretty, frilly, highly feminine garments. Where female clothing is out of reach, the boy's own items of clothing may be worn in a fashion which imitates a girl's belted overblouse, a young woman's slim waist, etc. Sometimes the result is displayed openly, in other cases the clothes are hidden in the boy's bed to be worn secretly at nighttime. When inter-

[17] These were observed in the Hampstead Child-Therapy Clinic during a diagnostic procedure or during analytic therapy.

fered with, the boy either rationalizes his behavior, or denies it guiltily, or even "cries pathetically," according to the mother's report, when the illegitimately acquired garments are taken off him.

External circumstances also resemble each other in the various cases. There is, almost without exception, some pressure toward femininity exerted from the side of the mother who openly prefers an elder or younger sister or admits that she wished for a girl before the boy was born. Or, as one boy of divorced parents expressed it, the mother "does not like men because she does not like Daddy." Frequently, there is collusion on the mother's part to the extent that she gives in to the boy's wish and buys his own frilly petticoats for him with the rationalization of "keeping the peace between brother and sister," etc. Separation from a loved female person (the mother, the beloved nursemaid) is another repeatedly found and obviously significant external circumstance.

In keeping with the overt behavior and the environmental influences, the various meanings of the transvestite procedures have been established in the boys' analyses. To dress up as a girl represents, for some, a bid for the mother's love in the disguise of the allegedly preferred sister. With others, it serves a complete denial of the boy's phallic masculinity which, rightly or wrongly, he imagines to be unwelcome to the mother. With others, again, it preserves the internal libidinal tie to a lost love object by partial identification with her.

It is true, of course, that, as in the girl's case, the boy's transvestite behavior is based on quantitative alterations in his libido economy. Without an excessive strengthening of feminine leanings, the boy's pride in his own masculine attire could not be overruled and other manifestations would have to be used to express the same envy, jealousy, rivalry, the wooing of the mother, the defense against separation anxiety, etc. Furthermore, the transvestite behavior in children of both sexes can probably be explained in terms of the child's fixation to a level on which part of the object is accepted as a substitute for the whole and on which, accordingly, easy displacements are made from the (male or female) body to the clothes which cover it, i.e., a fixation to the developmental phase in which the symbolism of clothes is rooted (Flugel, 1930).

As regards the prognostic significance of transvestite behavior, it need not be considered as more or as less ominous than any of the other expressions of a child's bisexual conflict or bisexual disharmony. Just as on the girl's side it is bound to the stage of penis envy, so it is bound on the boy's to the phase-determined femininity of the anal-passive period, to the negative oedipus complex or to regressions to these attitudes. So far as it serves the purpose of defense against anxiety (separation anxiety, fear of loss of love, phallic dangers), there is no reason to expect that it will persist longer than the phases in which these anxieties are uppermost. Only where the transvestite behavior is itself an outlet for the child's sexuality, i.e., where it is accompanied by unmistakable signs of sexual excitation, can it be considered as a true parallel to and forerunner of the perversion proper. Probably, those instances where the activity is pursued in secret, in bed and at night, are significant in this respect. But without direct proof supplied by erections, masturbatory activities, etc., in conjunction with it, the exact meaning of transvestitism in the sex life of the child is difficult to assess and verify, even in the cases under analysis.[18]

Fetishism

As shown in the foregoing sections, a child's overtly perverse behavior can be as much a part of his defense organization and his attempts at mastery as it is an expression of his sexual needs. This double aspect becomes even more obvious in the phenomena described as fetishism in children, which have received considerable attention in psychoanalytic literature.[19] Although there is much disagreement on essential points, most authors share the opinion that, although "childhood fetishism resembles fetishism in adults," the child's so-called fetish is "merely a stage in a process which may or may not lead to adult fetishism" (Sperling, 1963). Wulff (1946) expresses this very forcefully when he says that these "abnormal manifestations . . . in the preoedipal period are in their psychological structure nothing other than a simple reaction formation to an inhibited or ungratified instinctual impulse," or when he asserts that while "fetishistic manifestations in the young child are not at all uncommon," their psychological structure "is a different one" from adult fetishism. Here, as on occasions described above, it is obvious that using the same term for both the infantile and the adult manifestations leads to the erroneous assumption that the behavioral similarity between the two is matched by a corresponding metapsychological identity.

[18] In this connection see also Charles Sarnoff's discussion (1963) of Melitta Sperling's paper, "The Analysis of a Transvestite Boy."
[19] See Melitta Sperling (1963), "Fetishism in Children," with attached bibliography.

What the child has in common with the adult fetishist is the tendency to cathect some article or some part of his own or another person's body with large amounts of either narcissistic or object libido. On the strength of this cathexis, the article or body part assumes the status of a part object or need-fulfilling object and becomes indispensable to the individual. In adult psychopathology this situation is well known to the analyst. In the adult fetishist, the part object symbolized by the fetish has been recognized as the imaginary penis of the phallic mother to which the individual is tied for his sexual satisfaction. Concerning the passive homosexual I have made the point earlier that the male partner's penis itself can assume the status of a fetish, representing the individual's own masculine attributes which have become displaced onto the other man. Here too, sexual excitation and sexual gratification are tied indissolubly to the fetish, which is searched for compulsively and in the absence of which the individual feels starved of sexual satisfaction, deprived and castrated.

It is in this respect that the difference between the adult fetish proper and the child's overcathected fetishistic object becomes paramount. While the adult fetish serves a single purpose and plays a central role in the pervert's sex life, the fetishistic object of the child has a variety of symbolic meanings and serves a variety of id and ego purposes, both changing according to the phase of development which has been reached. At the time of suckling and weaning, for example, any article (such as a dummy, etc.) may become overcathected and indispensable, provided it serves on the one hand the infant's oral pleasure and on the other prevents or diminishes the arousal of separation anxiety by guaranteeing the uninterrupted permanency of gratification. According to Wulff (1946), the value of the fetish at this time lies in the fact that it "represents a substitute for the mother's body and in particular for the mother's breast." In a next stage, the overcathected article, usually in the form of a soft toy, a pillow, a blanket, etc., becomes a "transitional object" (Winnicott, 1953), charged equally with narcissistic and object libido which, for the purposes of libido distribution, bridges the gap between the child's own and the mother's person. According to Winnicott, these phenomena, although allowed and expected by the mother, are inherent in the child's own nature and as such are "part of normal emotional development." According to Melitta Sperling (1963), they are "pathological manifestations of a specific disturbance in object relationship" and are directly influenced and promoted by the mother's unconscious feelings and overt attitudes.

It is in the young child's difficulties at bedtime that these "transitional" or "fetishistic" objects play an especially helpful role in establishing the indispensable precondition for falling asleep, namely, the withdrawal of interest from the object world to the self. There are many children who are unable to go to sleep except in close proximity to such a treasured possession and who become deeply distressed whenever it is lost or mislaid; and on such occasions many mothers search for it frantically in answer to the child's obvious sense of deprivation. Melitta Sperling raises the question why a child should "become so addicted to an intrinsically valueless article that it becomes more important to him than the mother," and she concludes that this could not happen without the mother's active collusion. We arrive at a different answer if (in accordance with Winnicott) we give sufficient weight to the soothing properties of the transitional object in which the advantages of self-love are combined with the advantages of object love; furthermore, to its importance as a permanently controlled possession, in contrast to the mother, who is not under the child's control and whose independent coming and going, appearance and disappearance, threaten the child with feelings of insecurity and separation distress. Against the view that the mother has a role "in the genesis of fetishistic behavior and in the choice of fetish" (Sperling, 1963), it can be asserted that all the suggestions on her part would remain ineffective if they did not coincide with the child's own developmentally determined swings between autoerotism, narcissism, and object love.

There are many, more or less obvious, respects in which the fetishistic object is connected with other aspects of the child's polymorphously perverse sexuality. Specific qualities, such as texture, link the fetishistic object with the infant's early skin erotism, which it serves as an article to be rhythmically rubbed, stroked, touched, etc. Its smell, especially any kind of body smell, forms an important link with transvestite practices, which the fetish serves by determining the type of clothes, or underclothes, that are chosen for the dressing up. In the phase of anal sadism, the soft toy as transitional object serves the full expression of the child's heightened ambivalence by offering a safe outlet for the succession of loving and hostile feelings directed toward one and the same object. It is only during the phallic phase (Wulff, 1946) that the fetish finally becomes identified with the child's own, with the father's, or with the mother's imaginary penis.

How far this pseudo fetishism of childhood is a prestage and forerunner of the later real perversion remains an open question which, so far, no author has succeeded in answering to his satisfaction. Seen from the side of the analyses of relevant adult cases, there is no doubt of the early origin of their fetish and of its persistent nature, irrespective of the fact whether it is represented by a limb, a specific piece or type of clothing, shoe or glove, or, as in a particular case of fetishism in an adult,[20] by a noise, the first production of which could be traced back to the mother. Seen from the side of clinical experience with children, on the other hand, it is equally obvious that the number of childhood fetishes is far greater than that of the true fetishists of later years, which means that many of the infantile fetishistic phenomena are bound to particular developmental phases and disappear again when the special id or ego needs served by them have been outgrown.

As mentioned above in the case of transvestitism, the forms of the practice which are closest to the adult perversion and therefore most likely to persist are those in which, not the ego and defense concerns, but the instinctual needs are of first importance, i.e., those which, from the beginning, are accompanied by unmistakable signs of sexual excitation and serve as a major outlet around which the child's whole sexual life is organized. There also is no lack of such case descriptions in the literature.[21]

[20] Analyzed by the author.
[21] See Melitta Sperling (1963). A further illustration is the case of a four-year-old boy reported by Anna Freud and Sophie Dann (1951). This boy was an orphan, brought up without a substitute for the mother, and had turned to compulsive sucking and masturbating, autoerotism and fetishistic objects for his satisfactions. "When sucking, his whole passion was concentrated on face flannels or towels which he sucked while they were hanging on their hooks. . . . he treated the children's used bibs or feeders as so many fetishes, rubbing them rhythmically up and down his nose while sucking, treasuring all six feeders in his arms, or pressing one or more between his legs. When on a walk, he sometimes looked forward to these ecstasies with passionate excitement, rushing into the

Prediction of Outcome

In view of the many elements involved, it is not possible to predict with any accuracy the further fate of a component trend which has deviated from the norm in one of the described manners. It remains an open question whether the trend will take the normal course, finally, and come under the primacy of genitality, or whether it will remain independent and therefore become the nucleus of true perversion. There is no certainty about its ultimate fate before adolescence. Even then the outcome will depend on a number of influences such as the following:

whether the genital drive which sets in at puberty is strong or weak, i.e., capable or incapable of dominating the pregenital trends;

whether the amounts of libido which have remained behind at pregenital fixation points exert a regressive pull strong enough to interfere with and weaken genitality;

whether the progressive wish to be "big" and adult outweighs in the personality the regressive attraction of early satisfactions;

whether the object world offers opportunities for adult sexual gratification to the individual or whether the first genital moves meet with frustration, etc.

It is these quantitative factors added to the qualitative ones which make predictions of the final outcome difficult and unreliable.

---

nursery on coming home with the joyous exclamation 'Feeder— feeder!' " (p. 149). The boy's phallic excitation and masturbatory accompaniment were not in doubt. On the other hand, the fetish itself obviously had no phallic meaning, and the fact that he was indifferent to the same feeders when they were freshly laundered, suggested that his erotic excitement was derived from the smell probably connected with an early feeding situation.

CHAPTER 6

The Therapeutic Possibilities

In a psychoanalytic clinic for children,[1] the whole range of childhood disorders comes up for diagnosis, with a demand for treatment, beginning at one extreme end with the most common developmental difficulties, the educational failures and upsets, the delays and arrests in mental growth, and leading by way of the traumatized and seduced cases, and the infantile neuroses proper, to the other extreme of atypical grave ego defects, grave libido defects, borderline disturbances, autistic and psychotic states, delinquent or near-schizophrenic adolescents, etc.

With those accepted for child analysis, work alternates between therapy and fact finding, the two purposes taking precedence over each other in different degrees, at different times, and in different instances. There are cases where on closer acquaintance the therapist doubts that analysis need have been resorted to at all if preventive work with parents had been done at the right time, if the right educational

[1] Such as the Hampstead Child-Therapy Clinic.

213

opportunities had been created, or if the most harmful environmental interferences had been avoided. There are those where he feels as reasonably sure of the diagnosis as he feels of the appropriateness of the analytic method, if applied correctly. But there are also cases where the analyst is faced by nothing but enigmas, with no certainty about the therapeutic possibilities. In these last instances, he has to be content in the conviction that child analysis offers unrivaled opportunities for exploring their specific psychopathology. Obviously, no disturbance can be classified correctly or matched with the treatment of choice before the genetic, dynamic, and libido-economic factors responsible for it have been clarified.

Where analysis fails to bring about improvements, the blame is usually laid not on the psychopathology of the case as such, but on unfavorable external circumstances such as the therapist's lack of experience or skill, the parents' failure to cooperate, insufficient time being allowed for the analytic process, interruptions due to bodily illness, upsets in the home, change of therapist, etc. Where analysis succeeds, wholly or in part, its competence is taken for granted and we are not surprised enough that a definite and circumscribed procedure such as child analysis can benefit such a large range of disorders, in many instances totally different from each other so far as origin and structure are concerned.

THE CLASSICAL PSYCHOANALYTIC THERAPY FOR ADULTS: ITS RANGE AND DEFINITION

Psychoanalytic therapy was originally devised to fit the need of adult neurotics and, likewise, the first adaptation of the method to children was made with the infantile neuroses in mind.[2] Since then, in the adult field, the scope of analytic therapy has widened,[3] and, with minor alterations,[4] now serves, besides the neuroses, other categories of disturbances such as psychoses, perversions, addictions, delinquencies, etc. Again, child analysis followed suit extending its field of application in the same directions.

In adult psychoanalysis, we possess an extensive and constantly growing literature which deals with the psychoanalytic method, the elements contained in it, and the therapeutic processes set in motion by it.[5]

[2] Except for Melanie Klein and her followers who included severe ego defects and psychoses among their patients from the beginning.

[3] See the Symposium (1954) under this title.

[4] Or "parameters," according to K. R. Eissler (1953).

[5] Rather than quote the large number of individual authors, I list here a series of Symposia and Panel Discussions in which the subject is summed up:

1936 International Psycho-Analytical Congress, Marienbad: "The Theory of the Therapeutic Results of Psycho-Analysis" (Glover, Fenichel, Strachey, Bergler, Nunberg, E. Bibring). For the individual contributions see Symposium (1937).

1952 American Psychoanalytic Association, Midwinter Meeting, New York: "The Traditional Psychoanalytic Technique and Its Variations (Orr, Greenacre, Alexander, Weigert). For a report of the Panel Discussion, see Zetzel (1953). For the individual papers, see Panel (1954a).

1953 American Psychoanalytic Association, Annual Meeting, Los Angeles: "Psychoanalysis and Dynamic Psychotherapy" (E. Bibring, Gill, Alexander, Fromm-Reichmann, Rangell). For a report of the Panel Discussion, see Rangell (1954). For the individual papers, see Panel (1954b).

1954 Symposium held at Arden House, New York: "The Widening Scope of Indications for Psychoanalysis" (Stone, Jacobson, A. Freud). For the individual contributions, see Symposium (1954).

1957 Symposium, International Psycho-Analytical Congress, Paris: "Variations in Classical Psycho-Analytic Techniques" (Greenson, Loewenstein, Bouvet, Eissler, Reich, Nacht). For the individual contributions, see Symposium (1958).

We can extract from these publications a number of definitions of the aim of analytic therapy, such as the following:

that "it is one of the aims of analysis to change the interrelations between id, ego and superego" (Bibring [Symposium, 1937]);

that "analytic therapy induces the ego to stop or alter defences . . . , to tolerate id-derivatives which are less and less distorted" (Fenichel [Symposium, 1937]);

that "analysis influences the superego towards increasing tolerance" (Strachey [Symposium, 1937]);

that "the goal of analysis is an intrapsychic modification in the patient" (Gill [Panel, 1954b]);

that "the analyst's goal is to provide insight to the patient so that he may himself resolve his neurotic conflicts—thus effecting permanent changes in his ego, id, and superego, and thereby extending the power and the sovereignty of his ego" (Greenson [Symposium, 1958]).

There is complete unanimity among these authors (and many others not quoted here) that the main therapeutic effects of psychoanalysis are a change in the balance of strength between id, ego, and superego, an increase in their tolerance for each other's aims and, with this, of the harmony between them. This, of course, presupposes the assumption that, in the disturbances under treatment, intrapsychic conflict figures as the main pathogenic agent and that, compared with the paramount importance of this single factor, others such as, for example, faulty interpersonal relationships (R. Waelder [see Zetzel, 1953]), take second place. The therapeutic procedures are valued, then, according to the degree in which they serve this intervention.

PSYCHOANALYTIC THERAPY FOR CHILDREN: ITS RATIONALE

Although none of the pronouncements quoted above were made with child analysis in mind, they are nevertheless relevant for the child analyst since they prompt him to re-examine the preconditions of his clinical work and to determine the areas in which it is legitimate. What he has to define more closely are the relations between intrapsychic conflict, the psychopathology of childhood, and child analytic therapy. After all, to consider child analysis on a par[6] with adult analysis is justified only if the two methods, apart from technique, have a common field of application and common treatment aims.

Intrapsychic Conflict in Child Analysis

"NORMAL" CHILDHOOD CONFLICTS AND ANALYSIS

As discussed in previous chapters, intrapsychic conflicts as such are normal by-products of structural development, common to all individuals who have proceeded in growth beyond the primitive level of nondifferentiation. They arise as soon as ego and superego are sufficiently separated off, first from the id, subsequently from each other, each to pursue its own concerns.

Under normal conditions, these developmentally determined inner disharmonies are dealt with by the ego of the child himself, assisted by support, comfort, and guidance supplied by the parents. Where the latter is insufficient and the child's distress considerable, the help of child analysis

[6] See Chapter 2.

may be sought since clarification, verbalization and interpretation, used consistently, reduce anxieties as they arise,
dissolve crippling defenses before they become pathogenic,
and open up, or keep open, outlets for drive activity which
bring relief. This helps the child to maintain a better equilibrium while passing through the various stages of development and on this circumstance is based the frequently heard
claim that all children could benefit from analysis, not only
the overtly disturbed ones. Nevertheless, the child analyst
cannot escape the feeling that here a therapeutic method is
assigned a task which, by rights, should be carried out on
the one hand by the ego and on the other by the parents of
the child.

THE DEVELOPMENTAL DISTURBANCES AND ANALYSIS

The situation is different in those instances where an uneven
progression rate in drive and ego development seriously
upsets the internal balance in one direction or the other.[7]
As described before, children with accelerated ego and superego development experience extreme distress when faced
with their own cruel, aggressive oral and anal impulses.
Although these may be phase-adequate from the point of
view of drive maturation, they are not considered as such
from the divergent ego aspect, and defenses against them
are set in motion. Similar distress, for opposite reasons, has
been shown to arise where ego progression is slowed up in
comparison with that of the drives; the ego is unable, then,
to deal with the pregenital impulses which invade it.

Here too the decision whether or not to use psychoanalytic
therapy is not a clear-cut one. After all, id and ego progress

[7] See Chapter 4.

may again balance each other out even if left untreated. On the other hand, the imbalance may be excessive, and in that case its effects may remain and do permanent harm to character and personality. Child analysis is able to prevent this and, by mitigating the conflicts, to act not only as a therapeutic but as a preventive measure in the truest sense.

The diagnostician here finds himself faced with the difficult task of prejudging the outcome of a developmental process which is still uncompleted.

THE INFANTILE NEUROSES WITH CHILD ANALYSIS AS THE TREATMENT OF CHOICE

None of these difficult decisions come into question with regard to the infantile neuroses (Diagnostic Category 3), and in this therapeutic field the child analyst can feel at ease. With the conflicts of the oedipus complex as precipitating cause and the neurotic symptomatology explained by the classical formula of danger→anxiety→permanent regression to fixation point→rejection of reactivated pregenital impulses→defense→compromise formation, the infantile neuroses not only come nearest to the corresponding adult disturbances in metapsychological identity, they also offer the analyst a role within the treatment which is similar to the one he has with adults. He can assume the part of helpmate to the patient's ego, and under favorable conditions is accepted by the child as such.

The question from what age onward the child's ego is mature enough to wish for treatment can be answered for the infantile neuroses by reference to the fact of symptom formation: an ego which withstands the drives sufficiently to enforce neurotic compromises on them thereby proves the intention to maintain its position and that indicates, at least in theory, its willingness to accept outside help for doing so.

Despite the fact, discussed above, that suffering from symptoms is not the same diagnostic indicator in children as it is in adults, many neurotic children are motivated for therapy by suffering, i.e., by the bodily discomforts and pains caused by the psychological upsets of stomach and digestion, the skin eruptions, asthma, the headaches, sleep disturbances, etc.; in the phobias of school, street, or animals, by the loss of freedom of action, the inability to do what other children do, and the exclusion from their pleasures; in the rituals and obsessions, by the feeling of being at the mercy of an unknown and compelling force which prescribes senseless actions; etc.

Occasionally these feelings are openly verbalized by children as, for example, by a boy patient of four and a half years[8] saying to his analyst after an attack of his compulsive ritualistic behavior: "Now you can see at least what my worries force me to do," expressing thereby the utter helplessness felt by his own ego in the situation; or by a girl of six, in the throes of a severe school phobia, who said to her mother: "You know, it isn't that I don't want to go to school, I just can't"; or by a latency girl, the eldest in a large family, with character difficulties caused by penis envy, jealousy, masturbation guilt, who was found to sing to herself: "All the other children are good and only I am bad. Why am I so bad?" She, like the others, expressed thereby the gulf she felt to exist between her ideal of herself, her superego demands, and her helpless ego, together

[8] Treated analytically in the Hampstead Child-Therapy Clinic by Audrey Gavshon.

with the puzzlement why, on her own, she could do nothing to remedy the situation (see also Bornstein, 1951).

Naturally, the child analyst will not expect such insights to provide more for the child than an initial approach to therapy. Even apart from the normal interference by resistance and transference, they cannot be relied on to persist for any length of time with children, or to provide a safe background on which to base technique.

To split the ego into an observing and an observed portion comes to the help of adult patients over long periods of their analyses, assists them in the working through process, and is completely swept away only in the worst storms of the transference neurosis. This attitude in which one part of the ego is identified with the analyst, shares in his increasing understanding, and takes part in the therapeutic effort, was convincingly described by Richard Sterba (1934).

Such introspection, which is a normal ego capacity in the adult, is not present in children. Children do not scrutinize their thoughts and inner events, at least not unless they are obsessional. In the latter cases, this particular split is merely one among several other tendencies to be divided in themselves, such as heightened ambivalence, the inclination to isolate, the urge to exploit self-criticism and guilt for masochistic purposes, etc.; that is to say, in these cases, introspection serves pathological rather than constructive ends. Apart from these cases, children are not inclined to take themselves as the object of their own observation or to take stock honestly of the happenings in their own minds. Their natural inquisitiveness is directed away from the inner to the outer world and usually does not turn in the opposite direction until puberty, when in some specific types of juveniles[9] self-examination and excessive introspection may appear as painful ingredients of the adolescent process.

In the preoedipal, oedipal, and latency periods, this habitual lack of perceptivity for the inner world also serves the child's reluctance to experience any conflict consistently as intrapsychic. This is where the mechanism of externalization,[10] not only onto the analyst, comes into play. It is well known that many children, after transgressing in one way or another against their own inner standards, escape the resulting guilt feelings by provoking the parents to assume the role of critical or punishing authority, an externalization of conflict with the superego which is responsible for many of the child's otherwise unexplained acts of disobedience. This refers quite especially to latency children with an active masturbation conflict who, after each irruption and satisfaction of their sexual needs, cannot do enough to turn the adult world against themselves by provocative behavior. In the realm of dissociality as well, it is a familiar fact that a guilty conscience not only follows the delinquent act but very often precedes and motivates delinquency. In all these instances, being criticized, accused, or punished by an external agent acts as a relief from the internal conflict with the superego.

Conflicts with the drives are treated similarly. Dangerous tendencies of preoedipal and oedipal origin such as oral and anal impulses, unconscious death wishes against siblings, hostility against the rival parent are displaced and externalized or projected onto figures in the outer world; these are thereby turned into seducers and persecutors with whom the child can enter into an external battle. The mechanisms

[9] Not in the delinquent type, of course.
[10] See Chapter 2.

used here are well known from the infantile phobias (school, street, animals) in which, by displacement and externalization, the whole internal battleground is changed into an external one.

Unfortunately for the child analyst, this tendency to externalize internal conflicts has a definite bearing on the child's expectations with regard to therapy. Where the adult neurotic expects relief from changes within himself, which he is therefore willing to bring about, the child pins his hopes on the therapist's superior power to effect changes in the environment, so far as this has been used to personify the child's own conflicting inner agencies.[11] In this sense, a change of school, away from a dreaded teacher, is expected by the child to relieve what are, in truth, his guilt feelings; or separation from a "bad" companion, to put an end to temptations, ignoring the fact that these arise from the child's own impulses and sexual-aggressive fantasies; or the removal from bullying classmates, to remedy what are, in reality, the child's own passive-masochistic inclinations. The therapist who, correctly enough, refuses to accept this role which the patient tries to thrust on him easily changes in the child's estimation from a helpmate to an adversary.

Frequently enough, the parents are inclined to join their child in this preference for environmental rather than intra-psychic alterations.

The child's lack of introspection and his consequently diminished insight into the nature of his neurotic difficulties are not identical with those resistances against analysis which can be understood and interpreted within the frame-

[11] See Chapter 2, Resistances.

work of his emotional attachments and in the transference. Lack of introspection is a general ego attitude, characteristic of childhood and adhered to by the child as an effective deterrent against mental pain. It is only in identification with a trusted adult, and in alliance with him, that it is given up and reluctantly replaced by a more honest viewing of the inner world.

The objection may be raised here that denial of the intrapsychic nature of conflicts is not exclusive to the child but is used as a defense by many adults as well. This is true, but, fortunately for the analyst of adults, the individuals who use this particular defense are not those, usually, who chose to enter analytic treatment. If they operate on an infantile level in this respect, they also prefer to "cure" themselves by external means, namely, by acting, or rather acting out, in the environment. It is a special difficulty, reserved for the child analyst, that his patients have to submit to a procedure and meet demands which they have not chosen knowingly or of their own free will.

A SUBSPECIES OF THE INFANTILE NEUROSIS IN ANALYSIS[12]

Where the child does not solve his conflict with the drives by means of an infantile neurosis proper, but removes the disagreement by lowering his ego standards altogether (as it happens in the infantilisms, the nontypical disturbances, some dissocial reactions), he is content with his deterioration in the same manner in which adults are content with their perversion, delinquency, or criminality.[13] In the manner of the adult, the child then feels that analytic intervention is undesirable and a disturber of a peaceful inner

[12] See Diagnostic Category 4.
[13] See Chapter 4, Permanent Regressions.

state. This places the analyst in the paradoxical position that, to treat the child, he has to foster (and welcome) the very id-ego conflicts which he tries to solve when dealing with the infantile neuroses.

In the history of child analysis this particular constellation was twice taken seriously enough to justify the introduction of specific technical parameters. August Aichhorn (1925, 1923-1948), expressed the view that he could make no headway in the analytic treatment of juvenile delinquents so long as they revolted against the environment and him while agreeing with their own dissocial leanings. By fostering a (narcissistic) tie and identification first with himself as a person and then with his value system, he changed their own ego standards and thereby carried disharmony into their structure. In his own words, when this happened, "the delinquent had been changed (or changed back) into a neurotic" who could now respond to psychoanalytic therapy more or less according to the ordinary standards. In the sense used above, he regarded the presence of intrapsychic conflict as a *sine qua non* for the application of classical analysis.

The so-called "introductory phase," suggested by me in 1926, had a similar motive (besides providing a first entry into the child patient's private world). Although misunderstood by many colleagues as an "educational" intervention, i.e., a device to bring about unjustified transference improvements, its real aim was to alert the child to his own inner disharmonies by inducing an ego state favorable for their perception. The rationale underlying this was my contention that intrapsychic conflict has to be reintroduced within the structure and experienced by the child before its analytic interpretation can be accepted and become effective. In present-day work the consistent interpretation of defenses serves the same purpose of id-ego confrontation.

SUMMARY

It is obvious from the foregoing that with regard to all childhood *conflicts*, whether transitory and developmental, or permanent and neurotic proper, disturbance and analytic therapy are closely matched. Apart from the well-known initial transference improvements which should deceive neither analyst nor parents, it is usually possible to relate in detail the improvements as they are taking place to the consecutive interpretations of material, resistance (defense) and transference repetition, i.e., to analytic work in its strictest sense.

In the developmental disharmonies and difficulties, distress is lessened and arrests are counteracted when anxieties are clarified and interpreted; regressions are undone, i.e., kept temporary, and progression is reinstated with the analytic clarification of the danger situation which enforced them. In the infantile neuroses, anxiety attacks, bedtime rituals, daytime ceremonials are reduced or conquered with the interpretation of their unconscious content; touching compulsions disappear when either their connection with masturbation or the underlying aggressive fantasies are revealed; phobias give way to the unraveling in interpretation of the oedipal displacements which have created them; fixations to repressed traumatic events are loosened with the trauma being brought back to consciousness in memory or relived and interpreted in the transference.

In the symptomatology of the infantile neuroses, double damage is done to the drive derivatives as well as to the ego. The therapeutic counterpart of this is the double action of the analysis. Since defense interpretation alternates with content interpretation, relief is given in turn to the hard-pressed ego and the equally hard-pressed drive until what is unconscious in both is brought nearer to the surface, is verbalized, clarified, interpreted, and becomes part of the child's integrated personality.

Therapy of the Nonneurotic Disturbances

As we move away from the conflict-based neurotic disorders (Categories 1-4) to the arrests, defects, and deficiencies of development (Categories 5-6), the therapeutic process changes its nature even though child analysis is still applicable and effects improvements.

THE THERAPEUTIC ELEMENTS IN PSYCHOANALYSIS[14]

All authors writing on the subject agree that more elements are contained in the analytic method than the *interpretation* of transference and resistance, *the widening of consciousness* at the expense of the unconscious parts of id, ego, and superego, and the consequent increase in *ego dominance*. While these are its mainstay, there are also other elements, the presence of which is unavoidable even where it is unintended. *Verbalization* and *clarification* of the preconscious play a definite role, especially with children, in preparing the way for interpretation proper and in lessening the impact of anxiety which goes hand in hand with it. There are the elements of *suggestion* which are inevitable consequences of the analyst's temporary position of power and emotional importance in the patient's life; with children they are represented by the so-called

[14] See E. Bibring (1954).

"educational" side effects of analytic treatment. There is the patient's tendency to misuse the transference relationship for "*corrective emotional experience*," a tendency which is all the stronger, the greater the role of the analyst as a "new" object. Finally, there is *reassurance*, which in the child's case is inseparable from the presence of and close intimacy with a trusted adult.

Analysts are taught to guard against these nonanalytic ingredients in the method and to keep their action at a minimum, but in the last resort the choice of therapeutic process does not seem to lie with them but with their patients.

Ferenczi (1909, p. 55) quotes S. Freud as saying with regard to the neuroses: "We may treat a neurotic any way we like, he always treats himself . . . with transferences," i.e., by repeating his neurotic constellations rearranged around the person of the analyst. Another impression, frequently put into words by Freud, was the following: "However, and by whatever technical devices we attempt to hold our patients in analysis, they on their side cling to the treatment in different ways, each on the basis of his particular pathology: the hysteric by means of his passionate transference love and hate; the obsessional by investing the analyst with magic powers in which he then participates in the transference; the masochist for the sake of the imaginary suffering which he extracts from the treatment process; the sadist for the purpose of having an object within transference reach whom he can torture; the addict, because he makes the person of the analyst as indispensable to himself as the drug or alcohol to which he is committed."

With regard to ego pathology, K. R. Eissler (1950) similarly states that every individual patient reacts to the analytic technique in his own way and that from the parameters which he enforces on his analyst, his ego's deviation from the norm can be concluded. Paraphrasing this, it can be said here that the nature of a child's disturbance reveals itself via the specific therapeutic elements which he selects for therapeutic use when he is offered the full range of possibilities that are contained in child analysis.

SELECTION OF THERAPEUTIC ELEMENTS ACCORDING TO
DIAGNOSTIC CATEGORY

To apply these viewpoints in detail to the field of infantile psychopathology:

As shown above, the prestages of infantile neurosis and the infantile neuroses proper react fully to interpretations of resistance and transference, defense and content, i.e., to the truly analytic measures, which for them turn into therapeutic processes, in so far as they initiate alterations and achieve improvements. Neither suggestion nor reassurance, corrective experience or management play a part worth mentioning, provided that the therapist himself does not step out of his analytic role. If the neurotic child turns to them at all, he does so as an expression of resistance at times when escape from analysis is more important to him than to achieve insight. But none of them either singly or combined have a therapeutic effect on the infantile neurosis which approximates what the analyst requires of a cure. Even if symptomatic improvements are achieved by such means, as in child guidance and child psychotherapy, the balance of forces between the inner agencies remains unchanged by them.

In contrast to this, the nonneurotic cases single out for

benefiting from them sometimes one, sometimes another, sometimes a mixture of the subsidiary therapeutic elements, while the main analytic procedure may remain without effect or bring about undesirable results, or fade into the background altogether.

With *borderline* children, for example, the classical back and forth between transference, defense, and content analysis has consequences which differ from those it has with neurotic children. In the borderline children fantasy activity is prolific, distortion of the id derivatives minimal, and accordingly interpretation is easy and straightforward for the analyst. But the usual relief and improved ego control of the fantasy world do not follow. Instead, the very wording of the analytic interpretations is taken up by the patient and woven into a continued and increased flow of anxiety-arousing fantasy. Met by interpretation only, whether within or outside the transference material, the borderline child uses the opportunity to turn the relationship with the analyst into a kind of *folie à deux*, which is pleasurable for him and in accordance with his pathological needs, but unprofitable from the point of view of therapy. On the other hand, therapy is served for him by verbalization and clarification of internal and external dangers and frightening affects which are perceived preconsciously but which his weak and helpless ego, left to itself, cannot integrate and bring under secondary process dominance. Diagnostically therefore, the borderline quality of a case can be assessed from its negative therapeutic reaction to interpretation of the unconscious proper.

Children with grave *libido defects* relate to the analyst on the low level of object relationship on which they have been arrested, i.e., they transfer symbiotic or need-fulfilling attitudes, absence of object constancy, etc. Here, interpretation proper will not have the desired effect of restarting development except in cases of traumatic or initially neurotic origin of the arrest. Where the libido defect is due to severe early deprivation in object relations, interpretation of the transferred repetition has no therapeutic results. Instead, the child may answer to the intimacy of the analyst-patient relationship, which is favorable for the proliferation of libidinal attachment because of the frequency and long duration of contact, the lack of interruptions, the exclusion of disturbing rivals, etc. On the basis of this new and different emotional experience, the child may move forward to more appropriate levels of libido development, a therapeutic change set in motion within the outward setting of child analysis but on the basis of "corrective emotional experience."[15]

Intellectually retarded children usually suffer acutely from their archaic fears. Due to the immaturity of their ego functions, they lack orientation in and mastery of the inner and outer world alike, and the very intensity of anxiety in turn prevents further ego growth. In child analysis this vicious circle is interrupted, with the result that the child proceeds gradually along the developmental scale from archaic fears of complete annihilation, to separation anxiety, castration anxiety, fear of loss of love, guilt etc.

---

[15] Unlike the effect of analytic interpretation which is not restricted for the child by age or time of intervention, corrective emotional experience is limited by maturational considerations. It has to happen approximately within the same developmental phase in which the damage to the libidinal processes has taken place. Once such time limits have been overstepped, it is too late for correction.

But the therapeutic element responsible for improvement in these cases is the analyst's reassuring role, not his analytic one.

Even in cases with organic defect (birth injury, minor brain damage) improvements are brought about in the severe impairments of personality formation. Where a comparatively normal ego exerts excessive pressure on a very impoverished drive constellation, the child profits from the stimulation of fantasy and opening up of outlets for id derivatives which are by-products of the analytic situation. Where average drive activity is insufficiently controlled by an undeveloped ego, the analyst's role and action as "auxiliary ego," another by-product of analysis, come to the patient's help.

Disturbed adolescents involved in analysis answer to one after the other element of the process in quick succession, according to the needs of their mixed psychopathology. This has been described in a recent study of such cases from the aspect of the analyst's intentional quick variations of technique (K. R. Eissler, 1958). Here it is seen as a spontaneous process on the part of the patient, namely, the variation of his selection from available therapeutic elements, while on the part of the analyst the procedure remains the same.

CONCLUSIONS

Within the area of permanent regressions and fixed neurotic symptomatology, nothing will change the child except analysis which works for alteration in the balance of forces within the structure. Outside the area of the neuroses, the child's personality remains more fluid and open to a variety of influences as they are exerted in family life, in education, or in therapy.

Inherent potentialities of the infant are accelerated in development, or slowed up, according to the mother's involvement with them, or the absence of it. Unharmonious progress is balanced out if the parents libidinize lines on which the child lags behind instead of making the common mistake of giving the highly intelligent children more food for intelligence; talking to the particularly verbal; and giving the bodily active more opportunity for action.

Destructive tendencies which have become excessive due to defusion of libido and aggression are lessened and bound again, if libidinal attachments are promoted. The libidinal and aggressive processes themselves answer to the offer of an object for cathexis. Ego attitudes are changed where opportunities for identification are opened up, or superego pressure relieved by opportunity for suitable externalization. In short, the possibilities for beneficial intervention in the developmental realm are almost as unlimited as those for harmful interference with development, or as the variations of normality and abnormality themselves.

Some analysts, after intensive study of specific areas and periods of child development, have recently advocated that for certain types of infantile pathology it might be advantageous if disturbance and therapy were more closely matched; that with libidinally retarded children their autistic or symbiotic needs should be attended to before all else; that children who have experienced early maternal deprivation should be given the opportunity for corrective emotional experience (Augusta Alpert, 1959; Margaret Mahler, 1955). Following the same reasoning, ego-defective children might be offered exclusively the reassuring protection of an auxiliary ego which they seek; borderline children, the ego-strengthening methods of verbalization and clarification.

At first glance such specialization of therapy seems rational and economical since it cuts out the potential waste which arises if we use a complex procedure such as child analysis outside its legitimate field of the neuroses, i.e., for patients who partake of only a minor portion of it and concentrate on the less essential elements. But, on closer view, several objections come to mind against applying such proposals to a majority of cases.

One objection is that in actual experience few individual child patients present us with the pure clinical picture which, alone, would justify a therapy directed toward one specific factor. In most cases, the disturbances consist rather of mixtures and combinations of elements which contribute in varying degrees to the final pathological result: libido defects are accompanied by ego defects, or are followed by them; acutely traumatic influences combine with the influence of chronic detrimental situations; delinquent and neurotic features intermingle; so do borderline and atypical features with neurotic conflicts; except in the most severe cases, there are always normal as well as abnormal areas in a child's personality. It is this mixed psychopathology of childhood for which the comprehensive method of child analysis is needed. Only in child analysis proper is the whole range of therapeutic possibilities kept available for the patient, and all parts of him are given the chance on the one hand to reveal and on the other to cure themselves.

For the analyst's inquiring mind, it is a second, vital objection that fact finding about assessment is at an end when the analytic method is not used. We need to be absolutely certain of the classification of a given case before taking the choice of therapeutic element away from the patient and into our own hands, i.e., before limiting the chances of therapy to one single factor. As our skill in assessment stands today, however, such accuracy of diagnostic judgment seems to me an ideal to be realized not in our present state of knowledge but in the distant future.

Bibliography

Aichhorn, A. (1923-1948), *Delinquency and Child Guidance: Selected Papers*. New York: International Universities Press, 1965.

———— (1925), *Wayward Youth*. New York: Viking Press, 1935.

Alpert, A. (1959), Reversibility of Pathological Fixations Associated with Maternal Deprivation in Infancy. *The Psychoanalytic Study of the Child*, 14:169-185.*

Angel, A., *see* Katan, A.

Bibring, Edward (1936), The Development and Problems of the Theory of the Instincts. *Int. J. Psycho-Anal.*, 22:102-131, 1941.

———— (1937), On the Theory of the Therapeutic Results of Psycho-Analysis. *Int. J. Psycho-Anal.*, 18:170-189.

———— (1954), Psychoanalysis and the Dynamic Psychotherapies. *J. Amer. Psychoanal. Assn.*, 2:745-770.

Bibring, Grete L. (1940), Über eine orale Komponente der männlichen Inversion. *Int. Z. Psychoanal.*, 25:124-130.

* *The Psychoanalytic Study of the Child*, currently 19 Volumes, edited by Ruth S. Eissler, Anna Freud, Heinz Hartmann, Marianne Kris. New York: International Universities Press; London: Hogarth Press, 1945-1964.

Böhm, F. (1920), Beiträge zur Psychologie der Homosexualität. *Int. Z. Psychoanal.*, 6:297-319.

──── (1930), The Femininity Complex in Men. *Int. J. Psycho-Anal.*, 11:444-469.

──── (1933), Über zwei Typen von männlichen Homosexuellen. *Int. Z. Psychoanal.*, 19:499-506.

Bonnard, A. (1950), Environmental Backgrounds Conducive to the Production of Abnormal Behaviour and Character Structure, Including Delinquency. In: *Congrès International de Psychiatrie*. Paris: Hermann.

Bornstein, B. (1949), The Analysis of a Phobic Child. *The Psychoanalytic Study of the Child*, 3/4:181-226.

──── (1951), On Latency. *The Psychoanalytic Study of the Child*, 6:279-285.

Bowlby, J. (1944), *Forty-four Juvenile Thieves*. London: Baillière, Tindall & Cox, 1946.

──── (1960), Separation Anxiety. *Int. J. Psycho-Anal.*, 41:89-113.

──── Robertson, James & Rosenbluth, D. (1952), A Two-Year-Old Goes to Hospital. *The Psychoanalytic Study of the Child*, 7:82-94.

Breuer, J. & Freud, S. (1893), On the Psychical Mechanism of Hysterical Phenomena: Preliminary Communication. *Standard Edition*, 2:1-17.†

Brodey, W. M. (1964), On the Dynamics of Narcissism: I. Externalization and Early Ego Development. *The Psychoanalytic Study of the Child* (in press).

Bryan, D. (1930), Bisexuality. *Int. J. Psycho-Anal.*, 11:150-166.

Bühler, C. (1935), *From Birth to Maturity*. London: Routledge & Kegan Paul.

Burlingham, D. (1952), *Twins: A Study of Three Pairs of Identical Twins*. New York: International Universities Press.

──── Goldberger, A., & Lussier, A. (1955), Simultaneous Analysis of Mother and Child. *The Psychoanalytic Study of the Child*, 10:165-186.

† See footnote ‡.

DALY, C. D. (1928), Der Menstruationskomplex. *Imago*, 14:11-75.

———— (1943), The Role of Menstruation in Human Phylogenesis and Ontogenesis. *Int. J. Psycho-Anal.*, 24:151-170.

EISSLER, K. R. (1950), Ego-Psychological Implications of the Psychoanalytic Treatment of Delinquents. *The Psychoanalytic Study of the Child*, 5:97-121.

———— (1953), The Effect of the Structure of the Ego on Psychoanalytic Technique. *J. Amer. Psychoanal. Assn.*, 1:104-143.

———— (1958), Notes on Problems of Technique in the Psychoanalytic Treatment of Adolescents: With Some Remarks on Perversions. *The Psychoanalytic Study of the Child*, 13:223-254.

FENICHEL, O. (1936), The Symbolic Equation: Girl=Phallus. *The Collected Papers of Otto Fenichel*, 2:3-18. New York: W. W. Norton, 1954.

FERENCZI, S. (1909), Introjection and Transference. In: *Sex in Psychoanalysis*. New York: Basic Books, 1950, pp. 35-93.

———— (1911), On the Part Played by Homosexuality in the Pathogenesis of Paranoia. In: *Sex in Psychoanalysis*. New York: Basic Books, 1950, pp. 154-186.

———— (1914), The Nosology of Male Homosexuality (Homoerotism). *Sex in Psychoanalysis*. New York: Basic Books, 1950, pp. 296-318.

FLUGEL, J. C. (1930), *The Psychology of Clothes*. London: Hogarth Press.

FREUD, ANNA (1926-1945), *The Psycho-Analytical Treatment of Children*. London: Imago Publishing Co., 1946; New York: International Universities Press, 1955.

———— (1945), Indications for Child Analysis. *The Psychoanalytic Study of the Child*, 1:127-150.

———— (1946), The Psychoanalytic Study of Infantile Feeding Disturbances. *The Psychoanalytic Study of the Child*, 2:119-132.

———— (1949), Aggression in Relation to Emotional Development. *The Psychoanalytic Study of the Child*, 3/4:37-42.

———— (1951), Observations on Child Development. *The Psychoanalytic Study of the Child*, 6:18-30.

———— (1952), The Role of Bodily Illness in the Mental Life of Children. *The Psychoanalytic Study of the Child*, 7:69-81.

———— (1962), Assessment of Childhood Disturbances. *The Psychoanalytic Study of the Child*, 17:149-158.

———— & BURLINGHAM, D. (1943), *War and Children*. New York: International Universities Press.

———— ———— (1944), *Infants Without Families*. New York: International Universities Press.

———— & DANN, S. (1951), An Experiment in Group Upbringing. *The Psychoanalytic Study of the Child*, 6:127-168.

———— *see also* Robertson, Joyce; Levy, Kata.

FREUD, SIGMUND (1893), On the Psychical Mechanism of Hysterical Phenomena: A Lecture. *Standard Edition*, 3:25-39.‡

———— (1900), The Interpretation of Dreams. *Standard Edition*, 4 & 5.

———— (1905), Three Essays on the Theory of Sexuality. *Standard Edition*, 7:125-245.

———— (1907), The Sexual Enlightenment of Children. *Standard Edition*, 9:129-139.

———— (1909), Analysis of a Phobia in a Five-Year-Old Boy. *Standard Edition*, 10:5-149.

———— (1913), The Disposition to Obsessional Neurosis: A Contribution to the Problem of Choice of Neurosis. *Standard Edition*, 12:313-326.

———— (1914), On Narcissism: An Introduction. *Standard Edition*, 14:67-102.

———— (1916-1917 [1915-1917]), Introductory Lectures on Psycho-Analysis. *Standard Edition*, 15 & 16.

———— (1918 [1914]), From the History of an Infantile Neurosis. *Standard Edition*, 17:7-122.

‡ *The Standard Edition of the Complete Psychological Works of Sigmund Freud*, 24 Volumes, translated and edited by James Strachey. London: Hogarth Press and the Institute of Psycho-Analysis, 1953-

——— (1919), Preface to Reik's *Ritual: Psycho-Analytic Studies. Standard Edition,* 17:259-263.

——— (1922), Some Neurotic Mechanisms in Jealousy, Paranoia and Homosexuality. *Standard Edition,* 18:221-232.

——— (1924), A Short Account of Psycho-Analysis. *Standard Edition,* 19:189-209.

——— (1926 [1925]), Inhibitions, Symptoms and Anxiety. *Standard Edition,* 20:77-174.

——— (1927), The Future of an Illusion. *Standard Edition,* 21:5-56.

——— (1930 [1929]), Civilization and Its Discontents. *Standard Edition,* 21:64-145.

——— (1931), The Expert Opinion in the Halsmann Case. *Standard Edition,* 21:251-253.

——— (1932), New Introductory Lectures on Psycho-Analysis. *Standard Edition,* 22:3-182.

——— (1937), Analysis Terminable and Interminable. *Collected Papers,* 5:316-357. London: Hogarth Press, 1950.

——— see also Breuer, J.

GELEERD, E. R. (1958), Borderline States in Childhood and Adolescence. *The Psychoanalytic Study of the Child,* 13:279-295.

GILLESPIE, W. H. (1964), Symposium on Homosexuality. *Int. J. Psycho-Anal.,* 45:203-209.

GREENACRE, P. (1960), Considerations Regarding the Parent-Infant Relationship. *Int. J. Psycho-Anal.,* 41:571-584.

GYOMROI, E. L. (1963), The Analysis of a Young Concentration Camp Victim. *The Psychoanalytic Study of the Child,* 18:484-510.

HARTMANN, H. (1947), On Rational and Irrational Action. *Psychoanalysis and the Social Sciences,* 1:359-392. New York: International Universities Press.

——— (1950a), Psychoanalysis and Developmental Psychology. *The Psychoanalytic Study of the Child,* 5:7-17.

——— (1950b), Comments on the Psychoanalytic Theory of the Ego. *The Psychoanalytic Study of the Child,* 5:74-96.

HELLMAN, I., FRIEDMANN, O., & SHEPHEARD, E. (1960), Simultaneous Analysis of Mother and Child. *The Psychoanalytic Study of the Child*, 15:359-377.

HOFFER, W. (1950), Development of the Body Ego. *The Psychoanalytic Study of the Child*, 5:18-23.

―――― (1952), The Mutual Influences in the Development of Ego and Id: Earliest Stages. *The Psychoanalytic Study of the Child*, 7:31-41.

ISAKOWER, O. Personal communication.

JACOBSON, E. (1946), The Effect of Disappointment on Ego and Superego Formation in Normal and Depressive Development. *Psychoanal. Rev.*, 33:129-147.

JAMES, MARTIN (1960), Premature Ego Development: Some Observation upon Disturbances in the First Three Years of Life. *Int. J. Psycho-Anal.*, 41:288-294.

JAMES, T. E. (1962), *Child Law*. London: Sweet & Maxwell.

JONES, E. (1932), The Phallic Phase. *Papers on Psychoanalysis*. Baltimore: Williams & Wilkins, 1949, pp. 452-484.

KATAN, ANNY (1937), The Role of "Displacement" in Agoraphobia. *Int. J. Psycho-Anal.*, 32:41-50, 1951.

―――― (1961), Some Thoughts about the Role of Verbalization in Early Childhood. *The Psychoanalytic Study of the Child*, 16:184-188.

KLEIN, M. (1957), *Envy and Gratitude*. London: Tavistock Publications.

KRIS, E. (1950), Notes on the Development and on Some Current Problems of Psychoanalytic Child Psychology. *The Psychoanalytic Study of the Child*, 5:24-46.

―――― (1951), Opening Remarks on Psychoanalytic Child Psychology. *The Psychoanalytic Study of the Child*, 6:9-17.

LAFORGUE, R. (1936), La Névrose Familiale. *Rev. Franç. Psychanal.*, 9:327-359.

LAGACHE, D. (1950), Homosexuality and Jealousy. *Int. J. Psycho-Anal.*, 31:24-31.

LAMPL-DE GROOT, J. (1950), On Masturbation and Its Influence on General Development. *The Psychoanalytic Study of the Child*, 5:153-174.

LEVY, K. (1960), Simultaneous Analysis of a Mother and Her Adolescent Daughter: The Mother's Contribution to the Loosening of the Infantile Object Tie. With an Introduction by Anna Freud. *The Psychoanalytic Study of the Child*, 15:378-391.

LEWIN, B. D. (1933), The Body as Phallus. *Psychoanal. Quart.*, 2:24-47.

LITTLE, M. (1958), On Delusional Transference (Transference Psychosis). *Int. J. Psycho-Anal.*, 39:134-138.

LOEWENSTEIN, R. M. (1935), Phallic Passivity in Men. *Int. J. Psycho-Anal.*, 16:334-340.

MAHLER, M. S. (1952), On Child Psychosis and Schizophrenia: Autistic and Symbiotic Infantile Psychoses. *The Psychoanalytic Study of the Child*, 7:286-305.

―――― & GOSLINER, B. J. (1955), On Symbiotic Child Psychosis: Genetic, Dynamic and Restitutive Aspects. *The Psychoanalytic Study of the Child*, 10:195-212.

MICHAELS, J. J. (1955), *Disorders of Character: Persistent Enuresis, Juvenile Delinquency and Psychopathic Personality*. Springfield, Ill.: Charles C Thomas.

―――― (1958), Character Disorder and Acting upon Impulse. In: *Readings in Psychoanalytic Psychology*, ed. M. Levitt, New York: Appleton.

MURPHY, L. B. (1964), Some Aspects of the First Relationship. *Int. J. Psycho-Anal.*, 45:31-43.

NUNBERG, H. (1947), *Problems of Bisexuality as Reflected in Circumcision*. London: Imago Publishing Co., 1949.

PANEL (1954a), The Traditional Psychoanalytic Technique and Its Variations. *J. Amer. Psychoanal. Assn.*, 2:621-710.

―――― (1954b), Psychoanalysis and Dynamic Psychotherapies: Similarities and Differences. *J. Amer. Psychoanal. Assn.*, 2:711-797.

PASCHE, F. (1964), Symposium on Homosexuality. *Int. J. Psycho-Anal.*, 45:210-213.

PECK, N. (1962), Chronological Age and the Rehabilitative Process. Thesis, Criminal Law Division, Yale Law School, New Haven.

RANGELL, L. (1954), Panel Report: Psychoanalysis and Dynamic Psychotherapy—Similarities and Differences. *J. Amer. Psychoanal. Assn.*, 2:152-166.

ROBERTSON, JAMES (1958), *Young Children in Hospital.* London: Tavistock Publications; New York: Basic Books, 1959.

ROBERTSON, JOYCE (1956), A Mother's Observations on the Tonsillectomy of Her Four-Year-Old Daughter. With Comments by Anna Freud. *The Psychoanalytic Study of the Child,* 11:410-433.

———— (1962), Mothering as an Influence on Early Development. A Study of Well-Baby Clinic Records. *The Psychoanalytic Study of the Child,* 17:245-264.

SADGER, J. (1920), Psychopathia sexualis und innere Sekretion. *Fortschr. Med.,* 1.

———— (1921), *Die Lehre von den Geschlechtsverirrungen.* Leipzig & Vienna: Deuticke.

SARNOFF, C. (1963), Discussion of "The Analysis of a Transvestite Boy," by Melitta Sperling [Abstract of Meeting of the Psychoanalytic Association of New York]. *Psychoanal. Quart.,* 32:471.

SPERLING, M. (1963), Fetishism in Children. *Psychoanal. Quart.,* 32:374-392.

SPITZ, R. A. (1945), Hospitalism. *The Psychoanalytic Study of the Child,* 1:53-74.

———— (1946), Anaclitic Depression. *The Psychoanalytic Study of the Child,* 2:313-342.

SPRINCE, M. P. (1962), The Development of a Preoedipal Partnership between an Adolescent Girl and Her Mother. *The Psychoanalytic Study of the Child,* 17:418-450.

STERBA, R. (1934), The Fate of the Ego in Analytic Therapy. *Int. J. Psycho-Anal.,* 15:117-126.

SYMPOSIUM (1937), The Theory of the Therapeutic Results of Psycho-Analysis. *Int. J. Psycho-Anal.,* 18:125-189.

———— (1954), The Widening Scope of Judications for Psychoanalysis. *J. Amer. Psychoanal. Assn.,* 2:567-620.

———— (1958), Variations in Classical Psycho-Analytic Technique. *Int. J. Psycho-Anal.,* 39:200-242.

WEISS, E. (1925), Über eine noch nicht beschriebene Phase der Entwicklung zur heterosexuellen Liebe. *Int. Z. Psychoanal.,* 11:429-443.

WINNICOTT, D. W. (1949), *The Ordinary Devoted Mother and Her Baby.* London: Tavistock Publications.

—— (1953), Transitional Objects and Transitional Phenomena: A Study of the First Not-Me Possession. *Int. J. Psycho-Anal.,* 34:89-97.

—— (1955), Metapsychological and Clinical Aspects of Regression within the Psycho-Analytical Set-up. *Int. J. Psycho-Anal.,* 36:16-26.

—— (1960), The Theory of the Parent-Infant Relationship. *Int. J. Psycho-Anal.,* 41:585-595.

WULFF, M. (1941), A Case of Male Homosexuality. *Int. J. Psycho-Anal.,* 23:112-120, 1942.

—— (1946), Fetishism and Object Choice in Early Childhood. *Psychoanal. Quart.,* 15:450-471.

ZETZEL, E. R. (1953), Panel Report: The Traditional Psychoanalytic Technique and Its Variations. *J. Amer. Psychoanal. Assn.,* 1:526-537.

Index

Fantasy—*Continued*
   in borderline child, 127, 230
   cannibalistic, 160, 175
   of fatherless boy, 194
   finding lost object, 112
   incompatible with superego demands, 125
   interpretation, 226
   loosening of control over, 100-101
   oral, 144
   oral impregnation, 59, 71, 160
   paranoid, 43
   passive, 19, 185
   profusion, 127, 230
   rescue, 15
   and surface manifestations, 13
   concerning surgery, 60
   and symptom formation, 150
   typical, 15
   underlying play, 80, 91
   see also Family romance, Masturbation, Twin fantasies
Fantasy games, 29, 203
Father
   attitude to boy's oedipal strivings, 194
   excessive love and hate of, and homosexuality, 191
   infant's relation to, 186
   oedipal relation to, 65-66, 96; *see also* Oedipus complex
   see also Parents
Fatigue, 69, 108
   and regression, 102-103, 105
Fear
   of annihilation, 132, 231
   and anxiety, 133
   archaic, 161, 231-232
   of being poisoned, 17
   for body safety, 77
   of conscience (superego), 44, 132, 135, 231; *see also* Guilt
   of external world, 146
   of independence, 137-138
   of intake and output, 71
   of loss of love, 43-44, 132, 135, 206, 231
   of object loss, 40, 43
   of parental authority, 6-8, 115

   see also Anxiety, Child, Phobia, Punishment
Feeding, 7, 60, 74, 75, 79, 135, 193, 208
   to adult attitude to food, development, 63, 69-72
   breast vs. bottle, 56, 61, 70, 159
   demand vs. timed, 56, 70, 155, 168
   difficulties, 153, 155-156, 159, 161; *see also* Eating disturbance
   to rational eating, development, 69-72, 159
   return to early patterns, 103, 106
   self-, 70-71, 90, 117
   sudden advances, 99
   see also Eating, Food
Femininity, 80, 83, 189, 202, 203
   phase-determined, of boy, 206
   see also Girl
Fenichel, O., 191, 215, 216, 239
Ferenczi, S., 191, 228, 239
Fetishism, as diagnostic category in childhood, 197, 207-212; *see also* Symptoms
Fixation, 94, 109, 162
   to aggressive-sadistic trends, 188
   in anal phase, 15
   and fantasies, 15
   and homosexuality, 193, 195
   in oral phase, 17-18, 20
   to passive oral and anal trends, 188
   and regression, 95-96, 103-104, 109, 147
   and transvestite behavior, 206
   and traumatic events, 96, 276
   in urethral phase, 18
Fixation points, 95-96, 129, 138, 144
   absence of, in ego regression, 104
   assessment, 143-144
   pregenital, 150, 212
Flugel, J. C., 206, 239
Folie à deux, 47, 230
Food
   avoidance, 47, 77, 120, 160
   battle over, 70-72, 160
   child's behavior to, 20, 70-71